Programming
The
Human
BioComputer

John Cunningham Lilly, M.D.

Translated by Beverly A. Potter, Ph.D.

Programming
The
Human
BioComputer

John Cunningham Lilly, M.D.

Translated by Beverly A. Potter, Ph.D.

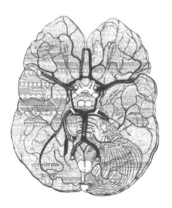

RONIN
Berkeley, CA

Programming the Human BioComputer

ISBN: 978-1-57951-065-7

Copyright © 1967, 1968 by John C. Lilly, M.D.

Derivative Copyright © 2004 by Beverly A. Potter &
                            Philip Hansen Bailey Lilly

Published by

RONIN Publishing, Inc.

PO Box 3436

Oakland, CA 94609

www.roninpub.com

Credits:

Translater:	**Beverly A. Potter, Ph.D.**	www.docpotter.com
Cover art:	**David Chabot**	CabotArt@cs.com
Cover design:	**Beverly A. Potter**	

Text fonts:	Times New Roman
	Zekton Delite by Ray Larabie
	Copperplate Gothic Bold by URW Software
	Gouty Old Style by URW Software

Distributed to the trade by **Publishers Group West**

Printed in the United States of America

Library of Congress Card Number 2004092086

Printing Number 2

Derived from *Programming and Metaprogramming in the Human Biocomputer,* by Beverly A. Potter, Ph.D.

Acknowledgements

THANK YOU TO LOVED ONES AND COLLEAGUES whose persevering presence made this edition possible, including Mary Louise Crouch Lilly, for her pioneering contributions in dolphin communication studies and the study of human consciousness.   Tony, loving wife and eternal friend. Colette and John Lilly, Jr. for their support and many efforts through many years. Patricia Sims for her unwavering intelligence and joy. Perrin and David Lilly for their understanding and longevity. Ann and Jerry Moss for their spirited kindness. Faustin Bray, Barbara Clarke Lilly, Lisa Lyon Lilly, Lili Townsend, Elsita Sterling,   Carol Bentley Ely, Jane Milatich, Judith Anderson, Lee Perry, Paradise Newland, Margaret Howe, Denise Smith, Char Raithaus, and Roberta Goodman, for their assistance, friendship, and love in the earthly and angelic realms. Brian Wallace and Glenn Perry for their, protection, service, poetry and music. Jay Shurley and Britton Chance for their research efforts contributing to the concepts discussed herein. Craig and Aliya Inglis for contributions above and beyond the call of duty. Jacques Mayol for his kindred spirit and love of the sea.   Jim Suhre, BigTwin, for developing and maintaining my www.johnclilly.com. Brumbear and Robyn for many years of friendship. Kim Kindersley, Napier Marten, and Robert Watts. Drs. Lawrence Raithaus, Joshua Trabulus, and Rick Perry. The International Cetacean Education Research Center—Kamala Hope Campbell, Takako Iwatani, and Claude Traks for their continuing efforts toward human, dolphin, and whale communication studies. The Institute of Eco-Technics, Pacific Coral Reef Foundation, The October Gallery, London, and the good ship, RV Heraclitus: John Allen, Tango, Gaye, Lazer, Chili, Cyclone, Francesco, Margaret Augustine, Gessie Houghton, ad infinitum, for your good works and presence on the planet. In Japan, Joichi Ito, Yasuhiko Suga, Kazuo Miyabe and Takashima Docpotter for her earthside translations. And Philip Hansen Bailey Lilly for his duty, honor, and grace

This edition is respectfully dedicated
to the memory of a dear friend,
son, brother and gentle soul,
Charles Richard Lilly.

Table of Contents

We shall meet somewhere in Alternity

Preface

PROGRAMMING THE H UMAN BIOCOMPUTER transmits methods by which a human can achieve stupendous feats of first, discovering our mind's extraordinary wishes and dreams and second, making them authentic by aligning them with the limiting reality of the human body—or bodies.

Lilly's book emerged from years of rigorous, intensive, even ruthless investigations of his mind confined in experimental-experiential conditions that went beyond even the walled-in fasting cave of the Tibetan master or the deep labyrinthine caves of the ancient shaman—namely the flotation tank, which eliminates input from other humans and from outer sense impressions as well as the effects of gravity on the nervous system.

Secondly, of course Lilly also used, as did the old masters, a refined self-observation and memory to note and record the slightest movements of state, percept or concept emerging from the inner cave. Thirdly, he did his work in a less paranoic era in which qualified investigators could freely obtain LSD, in Lilly's case through the US Navy, and so legal or emotional fears of persecution did not contaminate its use. LSD produced time dependent phenomena in nine hours that would take months of fasting in caves to achieve. Fourthly, Lilly dropped dependence upon sectarian metaphors of archetypes, gods, platonic forms, and geometries and developed the neutral metaphor of computer programs and metaprograms to

> This book possesses metaphysical integrity and charisma unparalleled in scientific culture.

which he added self-metaprograms, those which an "I" could operate. He boldly experimented with supra-self-programs that modeled various cosmologies and reduced his observational I to a microdot explorer free to travel anywhere in that world.

Lilly's experimental cosmos cannot be reduced to a page or so. I do suggest that this book possesses a metaphysical integrity and transmitting charisma unparalleled in scientific culture, although Lorenz's *Behind the Mirror* and the dynamics of chaos give useful background material. Lilly gives us a universal methodology stripped of ideological clothing to explore all mental phenomena.

His method and results vividly light up ultimate intricacies of Tantra, marvelous revelations of Gurdjieff about properties of the I, seven leveled Sufi teaching stories, and extraordinary discoveries of self-organizing complexity in physio-psychology about the nervous system, DNA, and hormones. Lilly's work stands alone, original, not a commentary on past masterpieces. This book is a treasure house through which any seeker after truth who insists upon not abandoning the scientific method and physical reality can find, staring one in the face, how to enter into a direct creative relationship with one's mind.

–John Allen
Biosphere 2

Introduction

HIS WORK HAS A CURIOUS HISTORY. It was conceived from a space rarer these days than it was in those days and written as a final summary report to a government agency–The National Institute of Mental Health. D'lysergic acid diethyl amide tartate was still "legal." The laws suspending scientific interest, research, involvement and decisions about that powerful entheogen were passed just as my initial research was completed. Researchers were inadequately consulted–put down, in fact. Legislators composed laws in an atmosphere of desperation. A negative PR campaign was launched nationally. LSD was the big scare–on a par with War, Pestilence, and Famine–as the destroyer of young brains, minds and fetuses.

In this atmosphere *Programming and Metaprogramming in The Human Biocomputer,* from which this current book evolved, was originally written. The work and its notes are dated from 1964 to 1966, but the conception was formed in 1949, when I was first exposed to computer design ideas by Britton Chance. I coupled these ideas back to my own software through the atmosphere of my neurophysiological research on cerebral cortex. My theories were more fully elaborated in the solitude of the isolation tank work at NIMH from 1953 to 1958, which ran in parallel with the neurophysiological research on the rewarding and punishing systems in the brain.

In this book you'll find general ideas from extrapolation and reworking of modern general purpose computer theory to explain and control some of the subjective operations of the human brain. An addition to the theory of the general-purpose computers, for the peculiarly human brain, is the concept of the self-metaprogram or the internal programmer present in the 10^{10} neuron assembly known as the human brain. Self-metaprograms operate between the huge storage and the huge external reality. Self-programming properties, in addition to stored program properties, are essential to understanding mental operations and resulting external general purpose behaviors such as speech and language. Stored programs and metaprograms are characteristic of the human.

The self-organizing aspects of computer programming and programs are conceptually reasonable and realizable in modern non-biological computers. The human brain, a super biocomputer is a parallel processor—a realizable artificial machine with this structure has not yet been built. This theory explains the actions of certain substances on the brain. Examination of stored programs and reprogramming are opened by the use of powerful entheogens—possibly by the introduction of small amounts of programmatic randomness, i.e., noise.

In the child, automatic metaprogram implantation or externally forced metaprogramming, persisting as metaprograms below the levels of awareness in the adult, can be controlling for the later adult programs, adult thinking, and adult behavior. Energy can be taken from some of these automatic metaprograms and transferred to the self-metaprogram with chemically evoked techniques and special central states. Some automatic unperceived programs are essential to biological nurture and survival. Examples of methods, of investigations and of results in self-analysis and self-metaprogramming are given.

Precautionary Attitude

WHILE I WAS WRITING THIS WORK in its original form, I was a bit too fearful to express candidly in writing the direct experience— uninterpreted. A group of thirty persons' salaries, a large research budget, a whole Institute's life depended on me and what I wrote. If I wrote the data up straight, I would have rocked the boats of several colleagues' and their family's lives—beyond my own stabilizer effectiveness threshold.

Despite my precautionary attitude, the circulation in 1967 of this work contributed to the withdrawal of research funds in 1968 from the research program on dolphins by one government

> I was a bit too fearful to express candidly in writing the direct experience— uninterpreted.

agency. I heard several negative stories regarding my brain and mind having been altered by LSD. At that point I closed the Institute and went to the Maryland Psychiatric Research Center to resume LSD research under government auspices where I introduced the ideas to the MPRC researchers. Later I went to the Esalen Institute in 1969.

At Esalen my involvement in direct human gut-to-gut communication and lack of involvement in administrative responsibility brought my courage to the sticking place. Meanwhile, Stewart Brand reviewed the work in the *Whole Earth Catalog* from a mimeographed copy I had given W. W. Harmon of Stanford for his Sufic purposes. Stewart wrote me asking for copies to sell. I had 300 printed photo-offset from the typed copy. He sold them in a few weeks and asked permission to reprint an enlarged version at a lower price. Skeptical about salability, I agreed. Bookpeople in Berkeley arranged the printing. Several thousand copies were sold.

Hidden Message

I HAD WRITTEN THE REPORT in such a way that its basic messages were hidden behind a heavy long introduction designed to stop the usual reader. Apparently once word got out, this device no longer stalled the interested readers. Somehow the basic messages were important enough to enough readers so that the work acquired an unexpected viability. This new edition was channeled through Beverly Potter (Docpotter), my earthside translator who contributed the summaries of Pavlovian and Skinnarian programming.

—John C. Lilly

Somewhere in Alternity

1

Human BioComputer

LL HUMAN BEINGS, all persons who reach adulthood in the world today—all of us— are programmed biocomputers. No one of us can escape our own nature as programmed entities. Each of us may be our programs, nothing more, nothing less.

Despite the great varieties of programs available, most of us have a limited set of programs. Many are built-in or hardwired. In the simpler basic biocomputers, programs are mostly built-in—from genetic codes to fully-formed organisms. The structure of our nervous system reflects its origins in simpler forms of organisms from sessile protozoans, sponges, corals through sea worms, reptiles and proto-mammals to primates to apes to early anthropoids to humanoids to man. As adults we continue to reproduce the patterns of function of action-reaction determined by necessities of survival, of adaptation to slow environmental changes, and of passing on the code to descendents.

> All of us are programmed biocomputers.

As the size and complexity of the nervous system and its bodily carrier increased, new levels of programmability appeared, not tied to survival and reproduction. Still, the built-in programs survived as a basic underlying context— excitable and inhabitable—for the new levels by the overlying control systems. Eventually, the cerebral cortex appeared as an expanding new high-level biocomputer controlling the lower levels of the nervous system—the hardwired programs. Learning and faster adaptation to a rapidly changing environment appeared for the first time. As this new cortex expanded over several millions of years, a critical size of cortex was reached a new capability emerged— *learning to learn*.

Learning to Learn

AS THE CRITICAL BRAIN-CORTEX SIZE EVOLVED, languages and its consequences appeared. In the process of learning to learn, we make models, use symbols, analogize, make metaphors. We invent and use language, mathematics, art, politics, business, and so on.

Learning to learn reduces the necessity of having to repeat certain symbols, metaphors, and models each time they are needed. I symbolize the underlying idea in these operations as *metaprogramming*. Metaprogramming appears at a critical cortical size—the cerebral computer must have a large enough number of interconnected circuits of sufficient quality for the operations of metaprogramming to exist in that biocomputer. Essentially, metaprogramming is an operation in which a central control system controls hundreds of thousands of programs operating simultaneously in parallel.

Self-Metaprogrammer

WHEN I SAY WE MAY BE OUR PROGRAMS, nothing more, nothing less, I mean the substrate, the basic substratum under all else of our metaprograms is our programs. All we are as humans is what is built-in, what has been acquired, and what we make of both of these. So we are the result of the program substrate—the self-metaprogrammer.

From several hundreds of thousands of the substrate programs comes an adaptable changing set of thousands of metaprograms. Out of the metaprograms as substrate comes something else—the controller, the steersman, the programmer in the biocomputer—the *self-metaprogrammer*. In a well-organized biocomputer, there is a critical control metaprogram labeled "I" for acting on other metaprograms and labeled "me" when acted upon by other metaprograms.

Most of us have several controllers or "selves"—self-metaprograms—which divide control among them, controlling in time parallel or in time series in sequences. One path for self-development is to centralize control of your biocomputer in your self-metaprogrammer, making the others into conscious executives subordinate to the single administrator—the single super-conscience self-metaprogrammer. With appropriate methods, centralizing of control—the elementary unification operation—is a realizable state for many, if not all biocomputers.

> We can program any conceivable model of the universe inside our own structure.

Supra-Self-Metaprograms

ABOVE AND BEYOND THE CONTROL HIERARCHY—the position of this single administrative self-metaprogrammer and its staff—there may be other controls and controllers called *supra-self-metaprograms*. These are many or one depending on current states of consciousness in the single self-metaprogrammer. These may be personified "as if" entities, treated as if a network for information transfer, or realized as an "as if self" traveling in the Universe to strange lands or dimensions or spaces. If we do a further unification operation on these supra-self-metaprograms, we may arrive at a concept labeled God—the Creator, the Starmaker—or whatever. At times we are tempted to pull together apparently independent supra-self sources into an "as if one." Certain states of consciousness result from and cause operation of this apparent unification phenomenon. I am not sure that we are quite ready to do this supra-self unification operation and have the result correspond fully to an objective reality.

General Purpose Computers

WE ARE GENERAL PURPOSE COMPUTERS that can program any conceivable model of the universe inside our own structure. Our general purpose computer can reduce the single self-metaprogrammer to a micro size and program it to travel through its own model as if that reality were real. This property is useful when we step outside it and see it for what it is—an immensely satisfying realization of the programmatic power of our biocomputer. To overvalue or to negate such experiences is not a necessary operation. To realize that we have this property is an important addition to our self-metaprogrammatic list of probables.

> *The general (purpose) computer is . . . a machine in which the operator can prescribe, for any internal state of the machine and for any given condition affecting it, what state it shall go to next . . . All behaviors are at the operator's disposal. A program . . . with the machine forms a mechanism that will show (any thinkable) behavior. This generalization has largely solved the main problem of the brain so far as its objective behavior is concerned; the nature of its subjective aspects may be left to the next generation, if only to reassure them that there are still major scientific worlds left to conquer.*
>
> —W. ROSS ASHBY
> "What Is Mind?"
> *Theories of the Mind*

Model of the Universe

WHEN WE CAN CONTROL HOW WE MODEL the universe inside our self we are able to vary the parameters satisfactorily. Our self may reflect this ability by changing appropriately to match the new property. The quality of our model of the universe is measured by how well it

In the province of the mind, what one believes to be true is true or becomes true

matches the real universe. There is no guarantee that our current model does match the reality, no matter how certain we feel about the high quality of the match. Feelings of awe, reverence, sacredness and certainty are also adaptable metaprograms, which can attach to any model—not just the best fitting one.

Modern science knows this. We know that merely because a culture generated a cosmology of a certain kind and worshipped with it, is no guarantee of goodness of fit with the real universe. Insofar as they are testable, we now proceed to test—rather than to worship—models of the universe. Feelings such as awe and reverence are recognized as biocomputer energy sources rather than as determinants of truth, i.e., of the goodness of fit of models versus realities. A pervasive feeling of certainty is recognized as a property of a state of consciousness, a special space, which may be indicative or suggestive but is no longer considered as a final judgement of a true fit. Even as we can travel inside the models inside our heads, so can we travel outside or be outside of our model of the universe—still inside our heads. In this metaprogram it is as if we join the creators—unite with God. Here we can so attenuate the self that it may disappear.

We can conceive of other supra-self metaprograms farther out than these, such in Olaf Stapledon's *The Starmaker*. Here the self joins other selves, touring the reaches of past and future time and of space, everywhere. The planet-wide consciousness joins into solar systems consciousness into galaxy-wide consciousness. Intergalactic sharing of consciousness fused into the mind of the universe finally faces its creator—the Starmaker. The universe's mind realizes that its creator knows its imperfections and will tear it down to start over, creating a more perfect universe.

No Limits

WHEN WE USE OUR BIOCOMPUTER IN THIS MANNER we discover profound truths about our self and our capabilities. The resulting states of being, of consciousness, teach us basic truth about our equipment.

In the province of the mind, what one believes to be true is true or becomes true—within certain limits—to be found experientially and experimentally. These limits are further beliefs to be transcended. In the mind, there are no limits. The province of the mind is the region of our models, of the alone self, of memory, of the metaprograms. What of the region that includes our body, other's bodies? Here there are definite limits.

Consensus Science

THERE IS ANOTHER KIND OF INFORMATION in the network of bodies, which includes our connection with others for bodily survival, procreation, and creation. In the province of connected minds, what the network believes to be true, either is true or becomes true within certain limits to be found experientially and experimentally. These limits are further beliefs to be transcended. In the network's mind there are no limits.

But, once again, the bodies of the network housing the minds, the ground on which they rest, the planet's surface, impose definite limits. These limits are to be found experientially and experimentally, agreed upon by special minds, and communicated to the network. The results are called *consensus science*.

Thus, so far, we have information without limits in one's mind and with agreed-upon limits—possibly unnecessary—in a network of minds. We also have information within definite limits within one's body and in a network of bodies on a planet.

Philosophical Puzzles

WITH THIS FORMULATION, our scientific problem can be stated very succinctly. Given a single body and a single mind that is physically isolated and confined in a completely controlled environment in true solitude, such as when in the isolation tank or other void space, can we satisfactorily account for all inputs and all outputs to and from this mind? Can the mind be truly isolated and confined? Given the properties of the software—the mind of the biocomputer—can we find, discover, or invent inputs and outputs not yet in our consensus science? Does this center of consciousness receive and transmit information by some form of unknown modes of communication? Or does this center of consciousness stay within the isolated biocomputer?

In *The Quiet Center* I posed the question of whether the mind is "contained" so that what we experience—no matter how far out—is actually created within the mind, versus the possibility that the mind is unlimited and boundless so that far out experiences are actually really occurring in some other reality or universe. Such questions are unanswerable in our current reality or at least we cannot answer them with our current scientific tools. The pondering is illuminating, nonetheless, if for no other reason than that it leads us to new unanswerable questions about our essential nature.

This work is the result of several years of personal effort at understanding the various paradoxes of the mind and the brain and their relationships. The basic premises presented in this work may help resolve some of the philosophical and theoretical difficulties which arise when we use other viewpoints and other basic beliefs.

Some of the major philosophical puzzles are concerned with existence of self, with the relation of the self to the brain, the self to the mind, and self to other minds, as well as the existence or nonexistence of an immortal part of the self, and the creation of and the belief in various powerful fantasies in these areas of thought.

Each of us may be our programs, nothing more, nothing less.

2
Inner
Realities

WE HUMAN BEINGS have a basic need for imagining wish-fulfillments. Our wishful thinking becomes interwoven among our best science and our best philosophy. We need certain kinds of ideals for the intellectual and emotional advancement of each of us. We also need ways of thinking which look as straight at the inner realities as at the physical-chemical-biological outer realities. We need truly objective philosophical analysis inside ourselves as well as outside ourselves. This work is a summary of my efforts to attain objectivity and impartiality with respect to these innermost realities.

We might well ask where is such theory applicable? Once mastered, it may be directly applied in self-analysis. If we remember that "self" is a feedback-cause with other human beings, we can start at this personal end of the system and achieve beginnings of inter-human analysis by analyzing our selves first. If successful, we may see our self operating in improved fashions with other people, as judged by our self and, much later, as judged by others.

> Science needs ways of thinking which look straight at the inner realities.

The reflections of our intellectual and emotional growth may be seen when operating in our inter-human transactions—with one's spouse, children, relatives, colleagues, and professional and business contacts.

General Scientists Needed

THE PERSONS WHO CAN UNDERSTAND AND ABSORB this kind of theory need understand over a broad intellectual and emotional front. They need understanding and training in depth in multiple fields of human endeavor. General scientists can probably understand it best. The scientists to whom I have presented this theory, evidenced an immediate understanding and an immediate grasping of the basic fundamentals and consequence of the theory.

A second group who have no difficulty with the computer aspects of the theory but who may have difficulty with the subjective aspects is that large group of young people who have become immersed in computer use and programming. A few of this group may have the necessary biological and psychoanalytic background to understand this viewpoint. Additional training in self-analysis itself may be given to these few. Classically trained psychoanalytic scientists may find this theory useful with further study of computer programming aspects.

For purposes of this discussion, a *general scientist* is a person trained in the scientific method and trained in watching one's own mind operate and correcting one's scientific as well as philosophical and pragmatic errors as a result of such observations. In a sense, general scientists are scientists who are willing to study more than just one narrow specialty in an attempt to grasp as much knowledge as they can under the circumstances from other fields than their own. General scientists have a grasp of symbolic logic and of mathematics that they apply to problems other than their scientific specialty.

As with most insights into the innermost realities, advantages of this viewpoint cannot be seen directly until this way of thinking is absorbed into your mind. Those in the psychoanalytic group may have difficulties because few of them are trained in the general purpose types of thinking involved in general purpose computers.

Multidisciplinary groups may have difficulties using this theory because each individual must absorb the necessary kinds of thinking and motivations involved in each of the fields represented. Members of such groups can motivate each other to do individual learning in these areas and can help each other learn in the various areas. But it is up to each responsible individual to absorb enough to gain understanding on the levels presented.

The thinking machinery itself is at stake here. I have found it possible to see that the properties and the operations of my mind in many different states can be accounted for somewhat more satisfactorily when the types of thinking I'm discussing have been absorbed and understood. With the resulting increased control over conscious thinking and preconscious computations, with the newly enhanced respect for my fixed unconscious—what I call "as if built-in-programs"—the integration of my self with the deeper inner realities becomes more satisfactory.

Working Hypothesis

Do NOT TAKE THIS VIEW OF THE MYSTERIES of alternative realities as definitive, final, completed, or closed—even though the theory is phrased in definite statements. Accept each definite statement as a working hypothesis. My aim is not to make a new final philosophy, a new religion, or another rigid way of approaching our intellectual life. My aim is to increase the flexibility, the power, and the objectivity of the mind and its knowledge of itself. We have come a long

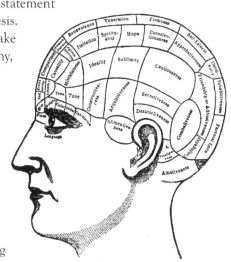

way from the lowly primate to our present level. But we have a long way to go. We have only to look at the inadequacies of Man's treatment of Man to see how far we must go if we are to survive as a progressing species with better control of our battling animalistic superstitious programs.

This theory will be useful in understanding and in programming your self as well as other minds. Enhancement of the very human depths of communication with other minds may be approached—hopefully it will. Hopefully the current limits and the attainable limits for education, for reprogramming, for therapy and for cooperative efforts of all sorts among others will also be approached. Time—and use of this kind of thinking—will test and shape a further working hypothesis.

Exploration of Inner Unknowns

I AM AN EXPLORER OF INNER UNKNOWN REALMS. My ambition is to be free to explore—not to exploit. I share what I experience because that is my profession—to search, to find, to discuss, and to write within science what I find. Let others use what I have found in their own professions, businesses, and pursuits. I have found that as soon as I go commercial or go political, I lose what I personally prize most—my objectivity, my dispassionate appraisal, my freedom to explore the mind within my own particular limits. To make money, to cure someone, to rule, to be elected, to grant money, to be a specialist in one science are all necessary and grand human enterprises needing persons of high intellectual and dedicated maturity. I am not one of those.

Each mind
is unique

To insist on the explorer's role in the region of Man's innermost mind is to insist on being intellectually unconventional and to espouse a region of research difficult to support. Grants for scientific research tend to be awarded by specialists to specialists. This is true in medical sciences as well as others. The material in this book cuts through too many specialties for that kind of support. Respect for the Unknown is hard to come by. Support for a science devoted to the innermost unknowns is needed.

Accept Unknowables

FOR CERTAIN KINDS OF PERSONS acceptance of unknowables and of the unknown itself is a great spur to work in this area. They have a powerful wish to push into the unknown further than those ahead of us in calendar time. Everyone has a notion about the truth in this area. Many other persons would like to have us follow their metaprograms. I prefer to be questing the mind and reporting on interesting journeys in that pursuit. So in that respect, I, too, am guilty of attempting to metaprogram the reader.

In summary then we start on the deeper journeys, independently, metaprogrammed properly, and relatively safe but without evasions. After having been through some of the innermost depths of self, a result is that they are only our own beliefs and their multitudes of randomized logical consequences deep down inside self. There is nothing else but stored experience.

3
What
Are We?

RE WE THE SUM AND SUBSTANCE of our experience, of our genetics, genetic inheritance, of our modeling of other humans, other animals and plants? Or are we something more? As we chip away at this major question of existence of self, as mankind has chipped away at this question over the millennia, we find that this question and the attempt to answer it lead to new understandings, new mathematics, new sciences, new points of view and new human activities. If we attempt to conceive of our self as having gone through another kind of evolution other than that of the human, if we attempt to conceive of ourselves as having lived in an environment different from the social one that we have been exposed to or if we attempt to imagine having evolved as an organism with the same or greater degree of intelligence in the sea or on a planet nearer to the sun or farther from the sun then we realize the essentially prejudiced nature of the self.

Let us carefully consider, for example, the genetic mutations leading to different human form, structure, function and mental set. One meta-theoretical position is that all such mutations in their proper combination exposed to the proper environment—of which there must be millions of possibilities—can survive and progress. In other words, even those mutations which are lethal here and now may have survival value under special new and different conditions. If there is any truth in this statement we should be doing experiments on adaptability and seeking the proper environment, proper peculiar diets, proper relation of sleep to wakefulness, light to dark, kinds and amounts of radiation, amount of noise, amount of motion, and so on for mutants at each stage in their life cycle. In other words, we should experiment with all of the vast parameters through which we have evolved and their variations to seek optimal survival values for the embryo, fetuses and children who do not survive under our peculiarly narrow range of values of these parameters. To change lethals to optimals seems possible and even probable with imagination and thorough research.

Test for Survival Power

OUR GENETIC CODE, with all its possible variations, is a general purpose construction kit for a vast set of organisms. We see only a few examples of what is possible in the adult human population in all races around the world. Through the exigencies of matings, of early embryonic development and growth, of the conditions imposed by mother, in her diet and physical and social surroundings, this molecular construction kit for organisms gives rise to organisms which test experimentally the conditions imposed upon them. They test how well the particular combination and particular values in their genetic code are combined to form an integral complete organism for coping with that particular environment and the particular organisms found in that environment, including bacteria and viruses.

I can conceive of an infinity of other environments populated with other viruses, bacteria, and complex organisms in which Humans could not survive in our present form. I can also conceive of our genetic code generating organisms which would survive and progress under those new conditions.

> Our genetic code is a general purpose construction kit.

Until we have thoroughly explored the genetic code to specify the organism and the conditions under which it can reach maturity to become an integral individual, we will not have the data necessary for specifying all of the characteristics of the human biocomputer which are brought to the adult from the sperm-egg combination.

Range of Adaptability

WE HAVE NOT TESTED our own range of adaptability as integral adults to all possible environments. Scientifically we have little experience with the extreme. We know something of the extremes of temperature, of air and of water in which we can survive. We know something of the radiation limits within which we can survive. We know something of the oxygen concentrations in the air that we breathe, we know something of the light levels within which we can function. We know a little of the sound levels in which we can function, and so forth. We are beginning to see how the environment interlocks with the human biocomputer to change its functioning. We are beginning to see how certain kinds of experiences with these conditions set up rules which we call "physical science" within our minds. We have seen when we change the external conditions in a limited way within a limited piece of apparatus, that the rules in our minds must be changed to understand how we can model these changed conditions and the way that atoms, molecules, radiation and space behave. Over the last century, we have seen a similar gain in our understanding of the operations of our minds, of the essential origins of thinking, and of those conditions under which we can elect to create new thinking machines within our minds.

This is an immensely difficult area for research.

We have begun to appreciate some of the powerful and special organizations of matter that are our essential organisms. The advances in the last hundred fifty years in biochemistry, in genetics, and in biophysics and molecular biology are the beginnings of a new control of these distributions of matter within ourselves.

Immortal Genetic Code

SCHRODINGER SAID THAT THE CHROMOSOME—which contains
the linear genetic code—is a linear two-dimensional solid.
Along its length it has a great strength and yet it is a
flexible chain that can move and can be split down the
middle during mitosis. These are carriers of the orders for
our ultimate structure as an integral adult. Their essential
immortality is being passed from one individual to the
next in creating the next individual in line and must be
included in any theory of the operation of our mind. It
may be that our individual unique basic beliefs can be
found by careful correlations between our essentially
unique genetic maps and our thinking limits. It may be
that the kinds and levels of thinking of which each of us
is capable are essentially determined by our genes. It may
be that our private languages are genetically determined.
Even if there is genetic determinism operating in our
thinking machines, we are far from specifying the levels of
abstraction and the cognitional and theoretical entities
that are genetically controlled.

If we can free ourselves from the effects of storage of
material from the external world on our
thinking machine and free ourselves from
the effects of stored metaprograms that
direct our thinking—programs devised by
others and fed to us during our
learning years—we may be able to see
the outline and the essential variables
that are genetically determined. This
is an immensely difficult area for
research. It requires that many
talented individuals consider their
own thinking processes, combined with a
detailed knowledge of their genetic structure and their genetic predecessors.

Genetic Determinism

OF COURSE IN THIS DISCUSSION we are entering into difficulties brought about by the phenotype-genotype differences. These will have to be taken into account as will all of the other mechanisms so laboriously worked out and discovered in the science of genetics. But rules of genetics must not be limiting in the meta-theory. They must enter as part of the knowledge of these talented individuals and at the correct level of abstraction for seeking the patterns of thinking which are genetically controlled.

Genetic determinism of thinking may turn out to be a will-of-the-wisp. It may be that in the subsequent development of the biocomputer it has become so general purpose that the original genetic factors and the genes are no longer of importance. Even as we can construct a very large computer of solid state parts or of vacuum tube parts or of biological parts, it makes little difference as long as the total size, the excellence of the connections and the kinds of connections are such that we can obtain a general purpose net result from the particular machine. So may we possibly cancel out genetic differences. So may each one of us attain the same kinds of learning and the same kind of thinking little modified by genetic differences.

Collaboration

I DO NOT WISH TO TAKE SIDES on these issues. I merely wish to say that if we are to take an impartial and dispassionate view, we cannot afford to espouse deeply any fixed pattern of thinking with regard to these matters. I would prefer to see talented individuals with large mental capabilities investigating their own minds to the very depths. I want to aid these individuals in their communication of the results to others, with similar yet different talents. I believe that by using certain methods and means, some of which are presented in this book, truly talented and dedicated individuals can forge, find, and devise new ways of looking at our minds—ways that are truly scientific, intellectually economical, and interactively creative.

Consider, for example, the case of the fictitious individual created by the group of mathematicians masquerading under a pseudonym. In order to create a mathematics or sets of mathematics beyond the capacity of any one individual, this group of mathematicians held meetings three times a year and exchanged ideas, then went off and worked separately. The resulting papers were published under the pseudonym, Dr. Nicholas Bourbaki, because the products of this work were felt to be a group result beyond any one individual's contribution.

Whether or not this group was greater than or lesser than a single human mind, operating in isolation on similar materials, will not be known for some time. It may be that the human biocomputer interlock achieved among these mathematicians created a new entity greater than any one of them in regard to modes of thinking, complexity of thinking, and creative new ideas. Certain kinds of things that Humans do of necessity require tremendous amounts of cooperation among very large numbers of individuals. Such accomplishments are beyond any one individual and are a product only of the group effort. This is true, for example, in building the Empire State Building, a subway system, a railroad system, an airline, a large industrial factory, and so on. In each of these cases there is a rearrangement of external realities, a setting up of a communication network between many individuals and a dedication of each of these individuals to the purposes of the organization of which they are a part. This is probably the greatest accomplishment of our industrial, military, educational and religious efforts. Man's effective interlock with other men can accomplish certain kinds of things beyond any individual.

Wasting Genius

IN CERTAIN AREAS, gifted, talented, intelligent individuals seem to function almost autonomously as solitudinous computers giving rise to new findings. This is seen in the case of the mathematical geniuses raised in isolation. One

is almost afraid to educate such people for fear that they will lose their general purpose nature and their ability to make original creative contributions.

Somehow or other they have escaped interlock into Man's ever more pervasive social organizations and their demands. As in the case of the creative physicist Moseley, who was drafted and killed in World War I, such talent can be thrown away by the necessary operations in our society.

There is a point of view in the modern world that we are wasting our use of talent and genius. There are antithetical philosophies that cause diversive intellectual activities. It may be that such conflict is necessary for the intellectual advancement of each individual. It may also be completely superfluous and nonsensical. C. P. Snow pointed out this kind of social dichotomy in his writings, especially those about the two cultures. The value systems of each intellectual reflect one's prejudices, biases, blindnesses, as well as areas of competence. It seems to be a very foolish maneuver to take that which one knows, that in which one is excellent and raise it above the general intellectual level of all other intellectuals. One technique of raising what we and our most intimate colleagues know above the surrounding intellectual terrain is to literally dig an intellectual moat around our field of activity. To dig this moat we demean and denigrate areas of knowledge and individuals in those fields surrounding our own field. This kind of activity seems to be almost built-in in our structure as biological organisms.

4
Theory

ACH MAMMALIAN BRAIN FUNCTIONS AS A COMPUTER, with properties, programs, and metaprograms partly to be defined and partly to be determined by observation. The human computer contains at least 13 billion active elements and hence is functionally and structurally larger than any artificially built computer of the present era. This human computer has the properties of modern artificial computers of large size, plus additional ones not yet achieved in the non-biological machines. This human computer has stored-program properties, and stored-metaprogram properties as well. Among other known properties are self-programming and self-metaprogramming. Programming codes and metaprogramming language are different for each human, depending upon the developmental, experimental, genetic, educational, accidental and self-chosen, variables, elements and values. Basically, the verbal forms are those of the native language of the individual, modulated by nonverbal language elements acquired in the same epochs of his development.

Each such computer has scales of self-measuration and self-evaluation. Constant and continuous computations are being done, giving aim and goal distance estimates of external reality performances and internal reality achievements.

Comparison scales are now set up between human computers for performance measures of each and of several in concert.

Each mammalian brain functions as a computer.

Each computer models other computers of importance to itself, beginning immediately postpartum, with greater or lesser degrees of error.

The relations of the activities of the brain to the subjective life in the mind have long been an arguable puzzle. Some advances in the reciprocal fields of study of each aspect of the question apparently can begin to clear up some of the dilemmas.

The sources of information I've used are mainly the results and syntheses of my experiments on the central nervous system (CNS). This includes the behavior of animals; the experiences and results of experiments I conducted in profound physical isolation, my personal psychoanalytic work on myself and others; my studies and experience with the design, construction, operation and programming of electronic solid state digital stored-program computers; my studies of analogue computers for the analysis and conversion of voice frequency spectra for man and for dolphin; the on-line computation of multiple continuous data sources; my studies and experiments in neuropsychopharmacology; my research on and with communication with humans, with dolphins, and with both. This has been combined with my study of certain literature in biology, logic, neuropsychopharmacology, brain and mind models, communication, psychoanalysis, computers, psychology, psychiatry, and hypnosis.

The introduction of an open-minded, multiple-level, continuously developing, on-line, operational, dynamic, economical, expanding, structural-functional, field-jumping, field-ignoring theory is needed. The applications of this theory extend from the atomic-molecular-membranes-cell levels though cell aggregational levels, total behavior and mental-cognitive levels of the single organism of large brain size to dyadic and larger groups of such individuals.

This is a report of a theory and its use which is intended to link operationally a) mental subjective aspects, b) neuronal circuit activities, c) biochemistry, and d) observable behavioral variables. Above all metaprograms, one metaprogram is of supreme value to me. My intent is to explore, to observe, to analyze. Hence there is an important additional basic metaprogram—analyze myself to understand my thinking and true motives more thoroughly. This is my conscious motivational strategy. At times this metaprogram domi-nates the scene, at times others do. My resolve exists, however, to generate a net effect with this instruction uppermost in the biocomputer hierarchy.

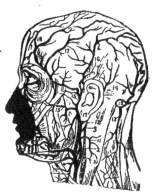

Basic Assumptions

THIS THEORY IS ROOTED in several basic assumptions. The human brain is assumed to be an immense biocomputer several thousands of times larger than any that we have constructed from non-biological components. The numbers of neurons in the human brain are variously estimated at 13 billions (1.3 times ten to the tenth) with approximately five times that many glial cells. The computer brain operates continuously throughout all of its parts and does literally millions of computations in parallel simulta-neously. It has approximately two million visual inputs and one hundred thousand acoustic inputs. It is hard to compare the operations of such a magnificent computer to any man-made machines because of its very advanced and sophisticated construction.

Certain properties of the human biocomputer are known, others are yet to be found. One is a very large memory storage. Another is control over hundreds of thousands of outputs in a coordinated and programmed fashion. Other examples are the storage and evocation of all those complex behaviors and perceptions known as speech, hearing and language. Certain programs are built-in, or hardwired, within the difficult-to-modify parts of the macro- and microstructure of the brain itself. At the lowest possible level, built-in programs are those of feed-ing, eating, sex, avoidance and approach programs, certain fears, pains, and so forth.

SCHEMA OF PROGRAMS

Level	Programs	Places
1	New, Modifiable	Neocortex
		Paleocortex
2	Old, Fixed Archeocortex	
3	Built-in	Subcortex

Permanence

PROGRAMS VARY IN THEIR PERMANENCE. Some are evanescent and erasable, others operate without change for tens of years. Among the evanescent and erasable programs we can categorize the ability to use visual projection in the service of our own thinking. This ability is found with a very high incidence among children and a very low incidence among adults. Handwriting, which maintains its own unique patterns for years is an example of a program operating without change for tens of years.

Lifelong Acquisition

PROGRAMS ARE ACQUIRABLE THROUGHOUT LIFE. No matter how old a person is, there is still a possibility of acquiring new habits. The difficulties of acquisition may increase with age, but the problem may not be so much with ability to acquire programs as a decrease in the motivation for doing so.

The young newly growing biocomputer acquires programs as its structure expands. Some of these take on the appearance of built-in permanence. Pronunciation of words is an example of such acquisition of programs in a child. Once it agrees with those of the parents the pronunciation is very difficult to change later. There is really no great motivation for the child to change a particular pronunciation when it is satisfactory to those who listen.

Inherited Genetic Code

SOME OF THE PROGRAMS of the young growing biocomputer are in the inherited genetic code. How these become active and to what extent is known only in a few bio-chemical-behavioral cases, at variance with the expectable and usual patterns of development. The so-called Mongol-oid phenomenon is inherited and develops at definite times in the individual's life. There are several other interesting clinical entities that appear to be genetically determined. To elicit the full potential of the young growing biocomputer requires special environments to avoid negative anti-growth kinds of programs being in-serted early in the young biocomputer.

The inherited genetic programs place the upper and the lower bounds on the total real performance and on the potential performance of the biocomputer at each instant of its life span. Once again we are assuming that the best environment is presented to the young organism at each stage of its life span. It is not meant to imply that such an environment currently is being achieved. This basic assumption seems highly probable but would be very difficult to test.

Creatability of Programs

INTERESTING AREAS OF RESEARCH are the erasability, modifi-ability, and creatability of programs. I am interested in the processes of finding metaprograms and methods and substances that control, change, and create the basic metaprograms of the human biocomputer.

It is not known whether we can really erase any program. Conflicting schools of thought go from the extremes that we store everything within the computer and never erase it to the other extreme that only the important aspects and functions are stored in the com-puter and hence, there is no problem of erasing. Modifi-cations of already existing programs can be done with more or less success. The creation of new programs is a difficult assignment. How can we recognize a new program once it is created? This new program may merely be a variation on already stored programs.

Some metaprograms are unsatisfactory. Educational methods for the very young is an example. It is doubtful if any metaprogram is fully satisfactory to the inquiring mind. Some are assumed to be provisionally enough. Belief in certain essential metaprograms is not easy. In a sense we are all victims of the previous metaprograms which have been laid down by other humans long before us.

General Purpose Computer

THE HUMAN BIOCOMPUTER has general purpose properties within its limits. The definition of general purpose implies the ability to attack problems that differ in quantitative degree of complexity as well as differing qualitatively in the levels of abstraction in the content dealt with. You can rapidly shift your mind and its attention from one area of human activity to another with very little delay in the reprogramming of your self to the new activity. The broader the front of such reprogramming the more general purpose the biocomputer is. The ability to move from the interhuman business world to the laboratory world of the scientist would be an example of a fairly general purpose biocomputer.

Stored Programs

THE HUMAN BIOCOMPUTER has stored program properties. A *stored program* is a set of instructions which are placed in the memory storage system of the biocomputer and which control the biocomputer when orders are given for that program to be activated. The activator can be another system within the same computer, or someone or some situation outside the biocomputer.

The human computer, within limits yet to be defined, has "self-programming" properties, and other persons-programming properties. This assumption follows naturally from the previous one but brings in the systems within

Systems & Storage

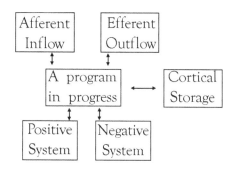

Data

New, current

Older

Inherited

Place

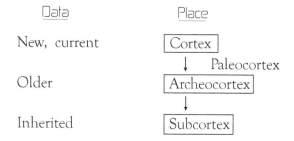

Schema of Programs

Level	Programs	Places
1	New, modifiable	Neocortex
	↕	↕ Paleocortex
2	Old, fixed	Archeocortex
	↕	↕
3	Built-in	Subcortex

the mind which operate at one level of abstraction above
that of programming. We literally must talk about self-
metaprogramming as well as self-programming. This does
not imply that the whole computer can be thought of as
the self. Only small portions of the systems operating at
a given instant are taken up by the self-metaprograms.
That is, there has to be room for the huge store of
programs themselves, of already built-in circuitry for
instinctual processes, and so on. All of these exist in
addition to others leaving only a portion of the circuitry
available for the self-metaprograms.

5

Self-
Metaprogramming

HE BIOCOMPUTER HAS self-metaprogramming properties, with limits determinable and to be determined. Self-metaprogramming is done consciously in meta-command language. The resulting programming then starts and continues below the threshold of awareness. Similarly, each biocomputer has a certain level of ability in metaprogramming others-not-self.

The older classifications of fields of human endeavor and of science are redefinable with this view of the human brain and the human mind. For example, the term "suggestibility" has often been used in a limited context of programming and of being programmed by someone outside. Hypnotic phenomena are seen when a given biocomputer allows itself to be more or less completely programmed by another one.

> The mind is the software of the biocomputer.

Metaprogramming is a more inclusive term than suggestibility. Metaprogramming considers sources, inputs, outputs, and central processes rather than just the end result of the process processes as shown in the table. Suggestibility names only the property of receiving orders and carrying them out rather than considering the sources, inputs, outputs, and central.

Primary State Induced
by Hypnosis & Entheogens

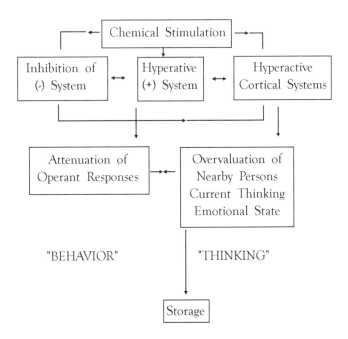

The Mind

THE MIND IS DEFINED as the sum total of all the programs and metaprograms of a given human biocomputer, whether or not they are immediately elicitable, detectable, and visibly operational to the self or to others. Stated another way, the mind includes unconscious and instinctual programs. This

> The mind is the sofeware and the brain is the hardware of the biocomputer.

definition and basic assumption has various heuristic advantages over the older terminologies and concepts. The mind-brain dichotomy is no longer necessary with this new set of definitions. The mind is the sum of the programs and metaprograms—the software of the human biocomputer—the hardware.

The Brain

THE BRAIN IS DEFINED as the visible palpable living set of structures to be included in the human computer. The biocomputer's real boundaries in the body such as bio-chemical and endocrinological feedback from target organs are yet to be fully described. The boundary of the brain, of course, may be considered as the limits of the extensions of the central nervous system into the periphery. We would include here the so-called autonomic nervous system as well as the central nervous system.

Third Entity

IN CERTAIN FIELDS OF HUMAN THINKING and endeavor, there is a necessity to have a third entity, sometimes including, sometimes not needing the brain-mind biocomputer. Theologians and other religious persons commonly define this entity as existing. Whether the term "spirit" or "soul" or another is used is immaterial. Such terms inevitably come up when discussing the meanings of existence, the origins of the brain-mind biocomputers and what happens to self after bodily death, and the possible existence of minds greater than ours.

This extra-brain-mind-computer entity can be included in this theory if and when needed. Such assumptions may be needed to give overall meaning to the whole of Man. Religion is an area for experimental science. Work starts in this area with the basic assumptions of the great psychologist, William James. Some compound term like "brain-mind-spirit-computer" may work. The problem of the existence theorem must be satisfied in regard to a third entity. There are some persons who assume it exists; there are others who assume it does not exist.

Programs are carried out by excitation-inhibition-disinhibition patterns among and in neural masses and sheets in the brain. Examples include the reticular activating-inhibiting system, the reward-punishment systems, and the cerebral-cortical conditionable systems.

Positive (+) and Negative I (-) Systems:
Short vs. Long Train Effects

Positive	Negative
Neocortex-long	Neocortex-long
Hippocampus-long	
Amygdala-long	
	Amygdala-long
	Intralaminar Thai. N-short
Caudate N-short	
Lat. Hypothalamic N-short	Med. Hypothalamic N-short
Med. Forebrain Bundle-short	
Interpeduncular N-short	
	Central Gray-short

The theory of the workings of the brain, mind and consciousness is not fixed or complete, but a beginning and put forth in the hope that it will serve as a foundation for others to build upon. As the theory grows, so may grow its accuracy and applicability. The theory should remain as open-minded as possible without sacrificing specificity in hazy generality.

Metaprogramming Language

THE COMMON "MACHINE-LANGUAGE" OF MAMMALIAN BRAINS is not yet discovered. The self-metaprogram language is a variation of the basic native language, yet unique in each specific human case. All of the levels and each level expressed in the self-metaprogram. Language for self-programming cover very large segments of the total operation of the computer, rather than details of its local operations. When certain concepts of the operation of biocomputers are effectively introduced into a given mind-brain-computer, their metaprograms can change rapidly. Language takes on a new precision and power in the programming process.

Stored Programs

CERTAIN SUBJECTIVE EXPERIENCES REVEAL ASPECTS of the operations of the biocomputer to the self. Changes in states of consciousness help delineate the bounds and the limits of the biocomputer's operations. Special techniques make it possible to inspect stored data and programs not normally available. Stored programs can be visualized, felt, heard, lived through or replayed, or otherwise elicited from memory storage by means of special techniques and special instructions. Evocation can be confined to one or any number of sensory modes, with or without simultaneous motor replay.

Desired attenuations, corrections, additions, and new creations with certain half-lives can be made after and even during evocation from storage, within certain limits. These can be done with half-lives in conscious awareness, and can be weakened or modified or replaced to a certain extent. An unmodifiable half-life can turn up for certain kinds of programs subjected to antithetical metaprograms. That is, orders to weaken, modify or replace a program act as antithetical metaprograms to already existing programs or metaprograms.

Conscious Awareness

ANOTHER BASIC ASSUMPTION is that new areas of conscious awareness can be developed, beyond the current conscious comprehension of the self. With courage, fortitude, and perseverance the previously experienced boundaries can be crossed into new territories of subjective awareness and experience. New knowledge, new problems, new puzzles are found in the innermost explorations. Some of these areas may seem to transcend the operations of the mind-brain-computer itself. In these areas there may be a need for meta-computer mappings. But first the evasions constructed by the biocomputer itself must be found, recognized, and reprogrammed. New knowledge often turns out to be merely old and hidden knowledge after mature contemplative analysis.

Some kinds of material evoked from data storage seem to have the property of passing back in time before the beginning of this brain to previous brains at their same stage of development. There seems to be a passing of specific information from past organisms through the genetic code to the present organism. But, again, this idea may be a convenient evasion to avoid deeper analysis of self. We cannot assume that data storage in memory goes back beyond the sperm-egg combination or even to the sperm-egg combination until a wishful fantasy constructed to avoid analyzing one's self ruthlessly and objectively is eliminated.

Intransigent Programs

APPARENTLY NOT ALL PROGRAMS ARE REVISABLE. The reasons seem various. Some are held by feedback established with other mind-brain-computers in the life-involvement necessary for procreation, financial survival, and practice of business or profession. Other non-revisable programs are those written in emergencies in the early growth years of the biocomputer. The programs dealing with survival of the young self sometimes seem to have been written in a hurry in disparate attempts to survive. These seem most intransigent.

Program Priority

PRIORITY LISTS OF PROGRAMS can function as metaprograms. Certain programs have more value than others. By making such lists the individual can find desired revision points for rewriting important metaprograms. In other words, it is important to determine what is important in your life.

> Certain programs have more value than others.

Psychoanalytic literature has described in great detail the basic bodily and mental function programs and their various forms dealt with in verbal-vocal modes-words, speech, grunts. Evasions, denial and repression are metaprograms dealing with the priority list of programs. Metaprograms to hide-repress-certain kinds of data storage material are commonly found in certain persons. Psychoanalysis and self-analysis are confined to the verbal-vocal-acoustic modes. Encounters with other persons in the real world have much more power to modify programs than either psychoanalysis or self-analysis. For example learning through sexual intercourse is more powerful than instructions given through the verbal-vocal mode.

Reward-Punishment

THE REWARD-PUNISHMENT DICHOTOMY OR SPECTRUM is critically important within the human biocomputer's operations. The detailed view of certain kinds of non-speech, nonverbal learning programs are exemplified in the work of Pavlov and of Skinner. Some of these results are the teaching and the learning of a simple code or language, a code with nonverbal elements (non-vocalized and non-acoustic) with autonomic components. Other motor outputs than the phonation apparatus are used.

6
Pavlovian
Programming

HE BASIC PRINCIPLES of classical programming were first discovered in Pavlov's experiments with dogs. The figure shows how this form of programming works.

At step one below Pavlov presented meat—the unprogrammed stimulus (UPS)—to a hungry dog. It is called unprogrammed because salivating at the smell of meat is built-in reflexive stimulus-response association. When the dog smelled the meat it responded with the unprogrammed response (UPR) of salivation. This stimulus-response association is part of the basic operating system of the dog's biocomputer. It can act as a basis for programming and metaprogramming.

Primary Plavlovian Programming

Step	Stimulus		Response
1	UPS ————————————→		UPR
	(meat)		(salivation)
2	PS + UPS ————————→		UPR
	(bell) (meat)		(salivation)
3	PS ————————————————→		PR
	(bell)		(salivation)

Pavlov demonstrated the programmability of the built-in salivation response when he rang a bell at the same time that he presented the meat to the dog. This is called "pairing," because the sound of the bell ringing was paired with the presentation of the meat. Again, the dog responded by salivating. Pavlov paired the sound of a ringing bell with the meat several times.

Next, Pavlov rang the bell but did not present the meat and the dog salivated anyway. The dog had been programmed to salivate at the sound of a bell. The bell is the programmed (PS) or learned stimulus and the salivation is the programmed (PR) or learned response as shown in step three. The association is called programming because dogs don't normally salivate at the sound of a bell.

Phobias & Emotional Reactions

PAVLOVIAN OR CLASSICAL PROGRAMMING is the process by which emotional reactions are programmed, including phobias or irrational fears as well as increased heart rate, rapid breathing, and sweating palms. For example, suppose you were riding a horse and it threw you off. Being thrown through the air would be the unprogrammed stimulus. The fear you experienced would be the unprogrammed response to flying helplessly through the air. As a result, you may very likely have been programmed to respond with fear to sitting on a horse—or possibly even to the sight of a horse—because of its *association* with the fear you experienced when thrown. Folk wisdom would tell you to get right back on the horse, because by doing so you can break the fearful association and thus unprogram or "extinguish" your fear of horses and riding them..

High-Order Programming

CONSIDER THE DOG ONCE AGAIN. In step four, Pavlov paired a light with the bell and the dog salivated. After repeating this procedure a number of times, the dog salivated at the sight of the light alone. This is called higher-order programming, because a programmed stimulus was used in the pairing.

Higher-Order Programming

4   PS(2)   +   PS(1) ——————→ PR(1)
        (light)   (bell)   (salivation)

5   PS(2) ————————————————→ PR(2)
        (light)   (salivation)

Most emotional reactions are learned through the process of higher-order programming. Suppose somebody has been programmed to respond anxiously to criticism. If this person is then criticized several times by the father, that individual may learn to respond anxiously in the father's presence, even when the father is not being critical, because the father has been paired with the aversive—unpleasant or painful—stimulus of criticism. Through higher-order programming, the father will probably become a programmed stimulus that elicits anxiety.

The emotional response, which some therapists might label neurotic, came about through higher-order programming because the stimulus (father) used in the pairing or programming is itself programmed, i.e., the person's anxious response to the father. Higher-order programming is one way in which some people acquire strong emotional reactions to certain minority groups or nationalities—even though they have had little or no personal contact with these groups. Higher-order programming also refers to the way in which words can have different connotations to different people.

Vague Anxiety

A PERSON NEED NOT BE AWARE OF THE PROCESS for programming to occur; nor is the selection of the programmed stimulus a conscious choice in most cases. *Anything that is present* in the situation when a person experiences an aversive stimulus, such as intense anxiety or panic, might become paired with that stimulus, and thus program the same emotional response. For example, in the case of the critical father, the room in which the critical remarks were made, such as his study, might also come to elicit anxiety in the person. When you understand the laws of programming you can employ these laws to metaprogram yourself in ways you choose.

People who experience a lot of vague anxiety might be programmed to respond with anxiety to many stimuli of which they are unaware. The color green might elicit anxiety in someone who, as a child, was severely spanked on a green carpet, for example. Small rooms might elicit anxiety because the spanking occurred in a small room, so that when in the presence of green or in a small room, this individual might feel vaguely anxious and be unaware that small rooms and the color green are eliciting this anxiety. Positive emotional responses to environmental stimuli are programmed in the same manner.

Higher-Order Emotional Programming

6      $PS(x) \longrightarrow PR(x)$
        (criticism)   (anxiety)

7      $PS(y) + PS(x) \longrightarrow PR(x)$
        (father) (criticism)   (anxiety)

8      $PS(y) \longrightarrow PR(y)$
        (father)   (anxiety)

In most cases programming will be extinguished or lose its hold on the individual if the unprogrammed stimulus is never again paired with the programmed stimulus. For example, in the case of the hungry dog, if the meat is never again paired with the bell, the dog will eventually stop salivating at the sound of the bell. When the pairing is sporadic—occurring infrequently and unpredictably—then the programmed response becomes "resistance to extinction" and persists.

Kinds of Stimuli

1. Physical specifications: end organs: kind and amount, timing, patterning of energy

2. Physiological specifications: neuronal: threshold values, patterns of neuron excitation (kind, place, impulses/ second) Central nervous system specification: number of excited neurons, where, what impulse frequencies; buildup of central state in what systems, its kind.

3. Central nervous system specification: Number of excited neurons, where, what impulse frequencies; buildup of central state in what systems, its kind.

Kinds of Responses

1. Patterned musculoskeletal

    (A) Starting a feedback pattern with apparatus or with another organism

    (B) Stopping a feedback pattern

2. Patterned CNS-biochemical states generating musculoskeletal responses:

    (A) Neutral

    (B) Net rewarding

    (C) Net punishing

    (D) Net ambivalent

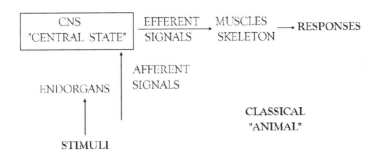

Self-Perpetuating

When the programmed response is anxiety or another strong negative emotion, the programming can become self-perpetuating because the sensation of anxiety is itself uncomfortable. Thus, when the programmed response is anxiety, the feeling of anxiety is continually paired with the programmed stimulus and is continually reprogramming the person. Thus, the person who was spanked on the green carpet might continue to respond with anxiety to the color green, even if such a punitive incident were never to occur again.

Generalization

Programming is not a static process; it may generalize or become more discriminative. Programming *generalizes* when a stimuli similar to the programmed stimulus take on the power to elicit the programmed response. The classic experiment that demonstrated this phenomenon was the case of an eleven-month-old child, "Little Albert." By repeatedly pairing a white rat with a loud noise—an unprogrammed stimulus—in front of Albert, his parent programmed Albert to cry—an unprogrammed fear response—at the sight of a white rat. The parents, who were psychologists, discovered that after the programming Albert also cried at the sight of other white furry things, such as a white rabbit, a white dog, and even Santa Claus. In this case, the programming "generalized" to several white furry and hairy objects.

Discrimination

Discrimination is essentially the opposite process. Discrimination occurs when the programmed stimulus elicits the programmed response *only under certain conditions*. Discriminative learning takes place when there is a third stimulus that is present each time the pairing occurs but that is not present when the pairing does not occur. For example, the anxious child may learn to discriminate among the critical father's expressions. The father is critical only when he frowns; but when he doesn't frown, he does not criticize. In this case, the child might be programmed to respond anxiously only when the father frowns.

A large fraction of the brain has stimulatable elements which give conditionable responses to local electrical stimulation at low levels.

1. Neocortex-projection systems (visual, acoustic, sensorimotor) present, now.

2. Paleo-archeocortex-fixed, old patterns.

3. Striate-mixed projection, positive-negative.

4. Hypothalamus-septum and mesencephalon—positive and negative-present.

7
Skinnerian Programming

B. F. SKINNER DISCOVERED the principles of operant programming, which is how most behaviors used in external reality are acquired. The principles of operant programming explain how operant or voluntary behaviors, such as hitting a baseball, typing, dancing, and even thinking are learned and how respondent behaviors, like anxiety or fear evoked through classical programming are maintained.

In operant programming the *consequence*—what happens immediately after the behavior—is crucial. Reinforcing consequences increase the likelihood that the behavior will recur, and punishing consequences reduce that likelihood. For example, a child might throw a tantrum in the presence of certain environmental cues such as being told to go to bed. The probability of the child throwing tantrums in the future will be determined by the consequences of that behavior. If the parent lets the child stay up late, then the tantrums will probably recur more frequently because throwing the tantrum was rewarded. On the other hand, if the child is reprimanded or deprived of a privilege—aversive consequences—his tantrums will probably recur less frequently.

BASIC PRINCIPLES

REINFORCEMENT IS A CONSEQUENCE *that makes a behavior more likely.*
Notice that the definition is based upon functionality. A
positive reinforcement occurs when something positive is
presented or "turned on" after a behavior. For example,
the parent who comforts a tantrum-throwing child is
positively reinforcing the tantrum behavior because comfort is a kind of positive attention that follows the
tantrum. If, on the other hand, the parent tells the child
that he doesn't have to go to bed now, the tantrum
behavior would be negatively reinforced because something
negative was removed or "turned off." That is, the child
did not have to go to bed.

	Something Positive	*Something Negative*
Present	Positive Reinforcement	Punishment
Withhold	Punishment	Negative Reinforcement

Punishment is a consequence that makes a behavior less likely.
There are two types of punishment. Positive punishment
occurs when something negative or unpleasant is presented
or turned on. By scolding the child, the parent would be
positively punishing tantrum behavior. Being scolded is a
negative event after the tantrum behavior. Negative punishment occurs when something positive is removed or
withheld—turned off. Depriving the child of a privilege
following a tantrum would be a punishment because
something positive is withheld as a consequence of throwing a tantrum.

Single Zone in "Motor" Cortex

(Noncortical)	Muscle response (to 1 pulse)
Move	Muscle response (to train)
Stop	Negative reinforcement threshold (conditioned avoidance)
Start	Positive reinforcement threshold (self-stimulation)
Alerting	Conditional stimulus (detection)

Subcortical Nuclei "Positive" Zone

Stop	(Spread to negative zone) muscle movements
Taming, Gentling	Autonomic responses
Start	Positive reinforcement (self-stimulation)
Alerting	Conditional stimulus threshold

SingleZone in "Negative" Subcortical Nuclei

Escape, Anger	Built-in somatic muscle patterns released
Fear	Autonomic responses
Stop	Negative reinforcement threshold (conditioned avoidance)
Alerting	Conditioned stimulus threshold

Threshold Current, at 30 ma
Second Train Durations

Threshold current
(Short Trains)

Threshold Current
(Ramp Schedule)

Establishing Cues

ANTECEDENTS ARE EVENTS OR STIMULI THAT SIGNAL that a certain behavior should be performed. Antecedent cues can be established in two ways. With respondent behaviors, the antecedent usually gains its power through classical programming or association. Recalling Pavlov's dogs, when an unprogrammed stimulus, such as the smell of meat, is paired repeatedly with a neutral one, such as a bell, the neutral stimulus will eventually elicit the salivation by itself. In other words, the bell becomes a cue that elicits the salivation. If this programmed salivation is then reinforced repeatedly by petting the dog or another positive consequence, the association between the bell and salivation will become permanent and it will not be necessary to pair the bell with the meat.

Little Albert provides another example. He was programmed to cry at the sight of a white rat because he associated it with a loud and frightening noise. This programming generalized to white rabbits, white dogs, and Santa Claus. Now suppose Little Albert sees a rat or a Santa Claus—the antecedent cue or programmed stimulus—and begins to cry—the learned or programmed response. Suppose when his mother hears him crying she gives him a lollipop. The mother's positive attention and the sweet taste of the lollipop are positive consequences. If this sequence were repeated a number of times, Albert would probably learn that the sight of a white rat or a Santa Claus is a cue to cry, because it is likely to bring his mother's attention and a lollipop. Thus, the power of the white rat—antecedent—to evoke crying—behavior—would have been programmed through classical programming and maintained with attention and lollipops—consequences—through operant programming. It would never again be necessary to pair the loud noise with the rat, because the crying behavior would be maintained by the reinforcement of receiving a lollipop from his mother.

> Behavior is influenced by what comes before it and by what follows it.

Motivational Hierarchy
of CNS Instructions

Most (+)	Lat. hypothalamus
	Ant. Med. Forebrain Bundle
	Orbitofrontal Cortex
	Amygdala
Least (+)	Entorhinal cortex
Neutral (0)	Septal Area
Negative (-)	Fornix

Antecedent cues are established by repeated association with a particular behavior-consequence sequence. When a behavior is consistently reinforced or punished in the presence of a particular stimulus, that stimulus becomes an antecedent that cues the person to the likely consequences of that behavior in that situation. Again, notice the use of functionality and probability.

Antecedent Power

ANTECEDENTS CAN BECOME SO POWERFUL that they can evoke certain behavior. For example, because ashtrays are usually present when one smokes cigarettes, the sight of an ashtray alone can evoke smoking behavior. Each time the smoker enjoys smoking after seeing an ashtray, the association is established even more firmly. In short, behavior is influenced by what comes before it and by what follows it. Antecedents "elicit" or "set the occasion" for the behavior to occur, and consequences "strengthen" or "weaken" the behavior response.

Stimulus Control

ESTABLISHMENT OF ANTECEDENT CUES is crucial in the development of stimulus control. This means that the likelihood of certain behaviors occurring is increased in the presence of some antecedents and decreased in the presence of others. For example, consider Jeff, a MaMa's boy. Suppose that when Jeff whines and makes excuses, his mother is sympathetic and comforts him; whereas when Jeff whines to his father, he responds with irritation and admonishes him to "act like a man." The mother's comfort reinforces Jeff's whining, while his father's admonishments punish whining. Quickly Jeff's whining behavior will come under stimulus control. The mother's presence becomes an antecedent that signals that whining is okay, while the father's presence becomes an antecedent that discourages whining.

Stimulus control is established through discriminative programming in which the individual learns that a particular behavior pattern, such as wearing sexy clothes, will be reinforced in the certain situations, such as when with friends at a party, but punished in others, such as when attending church. It is through stimulus control or discriminative programming that we learn what to do when and where and what to avoid doing—both in our interactions wit external reality and in our mental simulations.

Internal processes, including thoughts, desires, fantasies, images, feelings—just about any mental processes—are actually behaviors. They are actions that the biocomputer can engage in and are actions that can be programmed by the same principles revealed by the simple experiments with Pavlov's dogs and Little Albert's parents. this also applies to simulations on your mental screen.

Generalization

A PARTICULAR RESPONSE CAN GENERALIZE to more than one situation or cue. Generalization occurs when a particular behavior is reinforced or punished in the presence of a variety of cues. Generalization can also occur when a behavior is reinforced in the presence of a cue similar to but different from the original one. This is the way in which many children learn to respect people who wear uniforms, for example. A child might be praised for acting respectfully toward a police officer, and because a police officer's uniform is very similar to a fireman's uniform, the child might then act respectfully toward a fireman. After many such experiences, the child has been programmed to act respectfully toward anyone wearing a uniform. Over time, acting respectfully might generalize from people in uniform to anyone in a position of authority.

Feedback "Causes" in Central States

1. Patterns of immediate results of outside *stimuli*—strength, place, timing.

2. Patterns of immediate results of *responses.*

3. Stored integrated *consequences* patterns.

4. Continuous current cortical integration of selected past stored patterns and current results of outside *stimuli* and *responses.*

5. Cellular biochemical states of storage-depletion of specific substances in specific sites; reserves available in body.

6. Specific CNS biochemical states locally.

7. Built-in programs.

Accidental Juxtaposition

VARIOUS CENTRAL NERVOUS SYSTEM CIRCUITS existing as reward and as punishment systems when stimulated by artificial or by natural inputs must be taken into account. The powerful emotional underpinnings of "movement toward" and "movement away" must be included, as well as the acquisition of code symbols for these processes. Such symbols tend to set up the priority hierarchies of basic operational programs in micro-format-non-verbal-and in macro-format-verbal. Too often, accidental juxtaposition seems to key off improper hierarchical relations at the outset, with resulting priorities set by "first occurrence" spontaneous configurations, unplanned and unprepared.

With a new view and a new approach, proper program priorities could be set at the beginning of the biocomputer's life history with planned "spontaneities" graded by order of occurrence. The maintenance of general purpose properties from the early human years to adulthood is a worthwhile metaprogram.

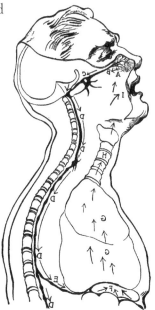

8
The Thinking Machine

 N GENERAL, THERE ARE TWO OPPOSING and different schools of thought on the basic origins of systems of thought or systems of mathematics—formalistic and unknowable sources.

Formalistic

THE FORMALISTIC SCHOOL OF THOUGHT makes the meta-theoretical assumption that a given system of thinking is based upon irreducible postulates—the basic beliefs of the systems. All consequences and all manipulations of the thinking machine are merely elaborations of or combinations of these assumptions operating upon data derived from the mind and from the external world. The formalistic school assumes that we can, with sufficiently sophisticated methods, find those postulates that are motivating and directing a given mind in its operations. A further meta-theoretical assumption is that once we find this set of postulates we will be able to account for all of the operations of that mind.

Unknowable Sources

THE SCHOOL AT THE OPPOSITE END OF A SPECTRUM makes the meta-theoretical assumption that thinking systems arise from intuitive mental operations that are essentially unknowable substrates. Among many other meta-theoretical ways of looking at our thinking machine and its activities is one which considers the unknown origins of basic beliefs and identifies those whose origins as unknown. In this view new kinds of thinking are created from unknown sources. Further, we are not able to arrive at all of the basic assumptions on which systems of thinking operate. Many of the assumptions are forever hidden from the thinker so that in this view underlying origins of thinking are wide open. With this meta-theoretical assumption we can conceive of presently inconceivable systems of thought existing in the future.

Integral System

THERE IS AN INTERMEDIATE POSITION between these two extremes in which we assume the existence of both sources of thought with each having something to offer. We can select thinking that is subject to formalistic analysis and formalistic synthesis based upon basic beliefs. But in doing so we realize that this does not include all thinking. Some thinking continues to be based in unknown areas, sources, and methods. In the integration view, meta-theoretical   selection is done by deliberate selection of the formal thinking from a large universe of other possibilities.   This position does not state that the origins of the basic beliefs are completely specifiable. Once basic beliefs exist, whatever their origin, a limited system of rules or combination of the basic beliefs, giving internally consistent logical results can be devised for limited use in that system. The process of organizing a limited integral system of thinking and selecting the basic beliefs that naturally fit into such systems of thinking is a way that Nature divides off this territory.

The problem of origin and the problem of how we construct basic beliefs is at stake here. If we take a naturally occurring thinking mind and obtain a sufficiently large sample of its thinking, we can have a meta-theoretical faith that we can then find the basic beliefs and their origins. I am not too sure that such meta-theoretical faith in our ability to adequately observe and record, and to adequately analyze our observations of mental events and construct them into logical explanations is warranted. With certain areas of thinking we can do this, with certain kinds of minds we can do this. But are not these the minds that have been organized along the known meta-theoretical pathways? Are not these the minds that believe implicitly in a basic set of beliefs and operate with them in an obvious direct logical fashion?

It may be better to conceive of minds and of criteria of excellence for general purpose minds in which we plug in meta-theoretical positions with multidisciplinary areas of applied formalism. Of course, in certain areas of thinking it is

> A given mind seen in pure culture by itself is the raw material for our investigation.

necessary to have a set of basic beliefs, including the rules of various games that we must play in the external physical and social reality. We can play these at different levels of abstraction with more or less excellence at playing, with or without dedication. Interlock with external reality has its own requirements, not just those of the mind itself. However, my interest is more in the unencumbered thinking machine itself. External reality is not a major emphasis in this discussion. The thinking machine's non-interlock structure can be studied during those times when the mind is unencumbered by external reality the necessities of interlock with other biocomputers. A given mind seen in pure culture by itself is the raw material for our investigation. The best laboratory for such observation is in profound physical isolation and in solitude—in the void space, which can be achieved in the floatation tank.

Systems & Storage

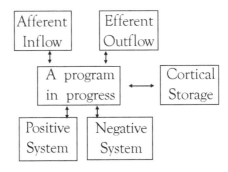

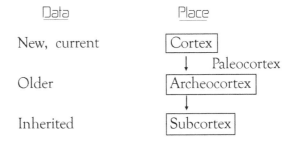

Schema of Programs

Level	Programs	Places
1	New, modifiable	Neocortex
	↕	↕ Paleocortex
2	Old, fixed	Archeocortex
	↕	↕
3	Built-in	Subcortex

Thus my major interests are in those meta-theoretical positions which remain as open as possible to reasonable explanation and reasonable models of the thinking processes, of the origins of beliefs, of the origins of self, the organization of self with respect to the rest of the mind, and the kinds of permissible transformations of self that are reversible, flexible, and introduce new and more effective ways of thinking.

Uniqueness of Each Mind

ONE FACT WHICH MUST BE APPRECIATED for applying this theory is the essential individual uniqueness of each of our minds, of each of our brains. It is no easy work to analyze one's self or someone else's. This theory is not, cannot be, a miracle key to a given human mind. It is devilishly hard work digging up enough of the basic facts and enough of the basic programs and metaprograms controlling each mind from within to change its poor operations into better ones. This theory can help us to sort out and arrange stored information and facts into more effective patterns for change. But the basic investigation of self or of other selves is not easy or fast. Our built-in prejudices, biases, repressions and denials fight against understanding. Our unconscious automatically controls our behavior. Eventually we may be able to progress farther. It may take several generations of those willing to work on these problems.

Within each level, each part has feedback-control relations with every other part as indicated by the connecting lines. Additionally each level has feedback-control with every other level. Many of these feedback connections are not shown for the sake of schematic simplicity. Some built-in survival programs have a representative at the supra-self-metaprogram level. The metaprogram: "These programs are necessary for survival. Attenuating or exciting them to extreme values should be avoided because such extremes lead to non-computed actions, penalties, illness, or death" is an example. After construction, such a metaprogram is trans-ferred by the self-metaprogram to the supra-self-metaprograms and to the supra-species-metaprograms for future control purposes.

The boundaries between the body and the external reality are between Levels I and II. Certain energies and materials—heat, light, sound, food, secretions, feces—pass this boundary in special places. Boundaries between body and brain are between Levels II and III. Special structures—blood vessels, nerve fibers, cerebrospinal fluid—pass this boundary. Levels IV through XI are in the brain circuitry and are the

Functional Organization of the Human Biocomputer

LEVEL		PARTS
XI	Above and in Biocomputer	Unknown
X	Beyond metaprogramming	Supra-Species-Metaprograms
IX	To be metaprogrammed	Supra-Self-Metaprograms
VIII	To metaprogram	Self-Metaprogram —awareness
VII	To program sets of programs	Metaprograms Metaprogram Storage
VI	Detailed instructions	Programs Program Storage
V	Details of instructions	Subroutines Subroutine Storage
IV	Signs of activity	Biochemical Activity—Neural Activity—Glial Activity—Vascular Activity
III	Brain	Biochemical Brain—Neural Brain—Glial Brain —Vascular Brain
II	Body	Biochemical Body—Sensory Body—Motor Body—Vascular Body
I	External reality	Biochemical—Chemical—Physical

software of the biocomputer. Levels above Level X are termed "Unknown" to maintain the openness of the system, to motivate future scientific research, to emphasize the necessity for unknown factors at all levels, to point out the heuristic nature of this schema, to emphasize unwillingness to subscribe to any dogmatic belief without testable reproducible data, and to encourage creative courageous imaginative investigation of unknown influences on and in human realties, inner and outer.

Limited Availability

SPECIAL USES OF THE HUMAN BIOCOMPUTER entail a principle of the competing use of the limited amount of total available apparatus. To hold and to display the accepted view of reality in all its detail and at the same time to program another state of consciousness is difficult. There just isn't enough human brain circuitry to do both jobs in detail perfectly. Therefore special conditions give the best use of the whole computer for exploring, displaying, and fully experiencing new states of consciousness. Physical isolation is one such condition. Physical isolation gives the fullest and most complete experiences of the internal explorations. Profound physical isolation can give new states of consciousness the "necessary low-level evenness of context" in which to develop. This is facilitated by minimizing the necessities for computing the present demands of the physical reality and its calculable present consequences-physical reality programs.

The principle of the competitive use of portions of the available brain explains why, for example, a large amount of hallucinating would not be permissible in our present society. If you are actively projecting visual images in three dimensions from stored programs, you may not have enough of your brain functioning in ordinary modes to deal with gravity, automobiles, and similar hazards, for example. You may become so involved in the projection in the visual field that the inputs from reality itself have to be sacrificed and their quality reduced. Apparently this danger teaches us as very young children to inhibit hallucinations—visual projection displays.

Size Matters

THE PRINCIPLE OF THE COMPETITIVE USE of available
biocomputer structure has a corollary. The larger the
biocomputer is, the larger the total number of
metaprograms and of programs storable, and the larger
the space that can be used for one or more of the
currently active programs simultaneously operating. The
larger the number of actable elements in the brain, the
greater the abilities to simultaneously deal with the
current reality program and to reinvoke a past stored-
reality program.   All other values being equal, the quality
of the details of the re-invoked program and the quality
of the operations in the current physical reality are a
direct function of the biocomputer's absolute functional
size.

There may be brains which are large enough to simultaneously project from data storage into the visual field while
functioning adequately in the outside environment. This is a
possibility—at least conceptually. This partition of the programs among various modes of operation is included in our
definition of the general purpose nature of a particular
biocomputer

Within certain limits, the "consciousness program" itself
is expandable and contractible within the biocomputer's
structure. In a coma, the consciousness program is nearly
inoperative, whereas in ordinary states
of awareness it requires a consider-
able percent of the machinery to
function. In expanded states of
consciousness the portion of the total
biocomputer devoted to its operation expands to a large
value. If the consciousness function is scrisorially expanded
maximally, there is little structure left for motoric initiation
of complex interaction and vice versa. If motor initiation is
expanded, the sensorial creations are reduced in scope. If
neither sensorial nor motor activities are expanded, more
room is available for cognition and feeling.

> The consciousness
> program is
> expandable and
> contractible.

The steady state values of the portions of the total biocomputer each devoted to a separate program at a given instant add up to the total value of one. The value of a given portion can fluctuate with time. The places used to perform these functions in the computer also change.

Metaprograms

METAPROGRAMS AND PROGRAMS COMPETE for the available circuitry. The methods of categorizing these competing programs depend on the observer's metaprograms. One system divides the competitors into visual, acoustic, proprioceptive, emotive, inhibitory, excitatory, disinhibitory, motor, reflexive, learned, appetitive, pleasurable, and painful. This system is used in neurophysiology and comparative physiology.

Psychoanalytic classification divides the competing metaprograms and programs into oral, anal, genital, defensive, sublimated, conscious, unconscious, libidinal, aggressive, repressive, substitutive, resistive, tactical, strategic, successful, unsuccessful, passive, feminine, active, masculine, pleasure, pain, regressive, progressive, fixated, ego, id, superego, ego ideal.

Humanitarians and intellectuals divide the metaprograms and programs into animal, humanistic, moral, ethical, financial, social, altruistic, professional, free,

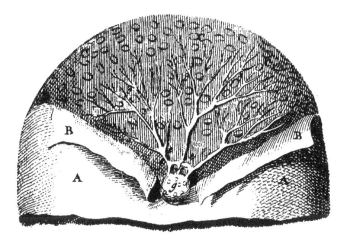

wealthy, poor, progressive, conservative, liberal, religious, powerful, weak, political, medical, legal, economical, national, local, engineering, scientific, mathematical, educational, humanistic, childlike, adolescent, mature, wise, foolish, superficial, deep, profound, thorough and so on.

Each classification of metaprograms and programs illustrate useful principles and help us better understand the human biocomputer. New systematizations are needed. The principles in this theory may be useful in setting up new schemas at each and every level of functioning of the biocomputer.

General Purpose Adaptability

THE ESSENTIAL FEATURES AND THE GOALS SOUGHT in self-analysis are in the metaprogram. In the general purpose nature of the biocomputer there can be no display, no acting, nor an ideal which is forbidden to a consciously-willed metaprogram. Nor is any display, acting or ideal made without being consciously metaprogrammed. In both cases we are up against the limits of the unique biocomputer which is one's own. There are certain kinds of metaprograms, displays, acting, or ideals which are beyond the capacity of a particular biocomputer. However, our imagined limits are sometimes smaller than those which we can achieve with special work. The metaprogram of the specific beliefs about the limits of self are at stake here. Ability to achieve certain special states of consciousness, for example, are generally preprogrammed by basic

> Our imagined limits tend to be smaller than those we can achieve with special work.

beliefs taken on in childhood. If the biocomputer is to maintain its general purpose nature—which presumably was there in childhood, we must recapture a far greater range of phenomena than we expect that we have available. For instance, we should be able to program in practically any area possible within human imagination, human action or human being.

No Ultimate Truths

AS EXPLORATIONS DEEPEN, we can see the evading nature of many programs which we previously considered basic to private and professional philosophy. As we open up the depths, it is wise not to privately or publicly espouse as ultimate any truths found in the universe in general, beings not human, thought transference, life after death, transmigration of souls, racial memories, species-jumping-thinking, nonphysical action at a distance, and other such revelations. Such ideas may merely be a reflection of survival needs. Ruthless self-analysis as to needs for certain kinds of ideas in these areas must be explored honestly and truthfully.

> We should be able to program in practically any area possible within human imagination, human action or human being.

After having done such deep analysis we later find deeper that these needs were generating these ideas. Our public need to proclaim them to self and to others, as if they are the ultimate truth, is an expression of the need to believe. Insight into the fact that we are enthused because the positive, start and maintain, rewarding sign has been chemically stamped on these ideas must be remembered.

An explorer operating at these depths cannot afford such childish baggage. These are disguises of and evasions of the ultimate dissolution of self. The maintenance of pleasure and of life are insisting on denial of death. If we stop at these beliefs, no progress in further analysis can be made. These beliefs are analysis dissolvers. They are lazy assumptions which prevent us from pushing deeper into self and avoid expending effort in this deeper direction. One very powerful evasion is an hedonistic acceptance of things as they are with conversion of most of them to a pleasant glow. Another evasion is deferring discussion of such basic issues such as life after death.

9

Science vs. Religion

NE CANNOT TAKE SIDES on these two widely diverse epistemological bases. On the one hand we have the basic assumptions of modern scientists and on the other hand the basic assumptions of those interested in the religious aspect of existence. If we are to remain philosophic and objective in this field, we must dispassionately survey both of these extreme meta-theoretical positions.

To become impartial, dispassionate, and general purpose, objective, and open-ended, we must test and adjust the level of credence in each of our sets of beliefs. If ever we humans are to be faced with real organisms with greater wisdom, greater intellect, greater minds than any single man has, then we must be open, unbiased, sensitive, general purpose, and dispassionate. Our needs for fantasies must be analyzed and seen for what they are and are not or we will be in even graver troubles than we are today.

> Our need for fantasies must be analyzed and seen for what they are and are not.

Our search for mentally healthy paths to human progress in the innermost realities depends upon progress in this area. Many men have floundered in this area of belief. I hope this work can help to find a way through one of our stickiest intellectual-emotional regions.

Most of these beliefs have been abandoned in the fields of endeavor called "science". While such beliefs continue to be found in the field known as religion.

Some of these beliefs are labeled in modem, psychiatric medicine and anthropology as "superstitions" or "psychotic" beliefs. Other persons present these beliefs in the writings called "science fiction".

Common Sense

POSSIBLY ONE OF THE SAFEST POSITIONS to take with regard to all of these phenomena is the formalistic view which assumes that the biocomputer itself generates all of the phenomena experienced. This so-called common sense assumption is an acceptable assumption of modern science and acceptable to colleagues in science.

Such considerations, of course, do not touch upon nor prove the validity or invalidity of the assumptions nor of the results of the experiments. To leave this theory open-ended and to allow for the presence of the unknown, it is necessary to take the ontological and epistemological position that we cannot know as a result of this kind of solitudinous experiment whether or not the phenomena are explicable only by non-biocomputer interventions or only by happenings within the biocomputer itself, or both.

This point of view assumes that if one plugs the proper beliefs into the metaprogrammatic levels of the biocomputer that the computer will then construct from the myriads of elements in memory those experiences that fit this particular set of rules. Programs will be run off and displays made which are appropriate to the basic assumptions and their stored programming. Obviously this point of view does not test the "objective" validity of the experiences.

Another approach is to start out with a basic set of beliefs, accept them to be "objectively" valid—not just "formally" valid—and do the experiments and interpret them with this point of view. If we proceed along these lines, we quickly reach the end of our ability to interpret the results. We find that we cannot grasp conceptually the phenomena that ensue. With this meta-theory, this type of experience is not just the computer operating in isolation, confinement and solitude on preprogrammed material being elicited from memory. But the biocomputer is really in communication with other beings, and the influence on one's self by them is real.

Thus in this case we are assuming the existence theorem in regard to the basic assumptions. That is, we assume that there is objective validity to the beliefs quite outside of self and our making the assumptions. This epistemological position can also be investigated by these methods. This is somewhat the position that was taken by Aldous Huxley and by various other groups pursuing certain non-Western philosophies as the *Ultimate Truth*.

Be Dispassionate

A BASIC LESSON LEARNED FROM THESE EXPERIMENTS is that, in general, our preferences for various kinds of meta-theoretical positions are dictated by considerations other than our ideals of impartiality, objectivity, and a dispassionate view. The meta-theoretical position held by scientists in general is espoused for purposes of defining the truth, for purposes of understanding in their particular compartment of science, for acceptance among other scientists and for each our internal security operations with respect to our unconscious programs. It is to be expected that anxiety is engendered in some scientists by making the above assumptions "as if true" in an experimental framework. We can easily be panicked by the invasion of the self-metaprograms by automatic existence programs from below the level of our awareness, programs which may strike at the existence of self, at the control of self, at the origins of self, at the destinations of self, and of the relations of self to a known external reality.

I wish to emphasize the necessity not to espouse a truth simply because it is safe. Being driven to a set of assumptions because we are afraid of another set and their consequences is the most passionate and nonobjective kind of philosophy. Too many intellectuals and scientists—almost unconsciously—use basic assumptions as defenses against their fears of other assumptions and their consequences. Until we can train ourselves to be dispassionate and accept both the assumptions and the results of making them without arrogance, without pride, without misplaced enthusiasm, without fear, without panic, without anger, hence, without emotional involvement in the results or in the theories, we cannot advance the inner science of Homo sapien very far.

Those who wish to embrace the truth of an alternative set of assumptions as an escape from the basic assumptions of modern science are equally at fault. Those who must find a communication with other beings in this kind of experiment will apparently find it. We must be aware that there are needs within one's self—just as in a child—for finding certain kinds of phenomena and espousing them as the ultimate truth. Such childlike needs dictate their own metaprograms.

Let the Data Speak

I AM NOT AGREEING WITH ANY EXTREME GROUP in interpreting these results. It is convenient for me to assume, as of this time, that these phenomena all occurred within the biocomputer. I tend to assume that ESP cannot have played a role. This is the position which I find to be most tenable in a logical sense. I do not wish to be dogmatic about this. I wish to indicate that this is where I stand at particular stage of the work. I await demonstrations of the validity of alternative existence theorems. If ever good, hard-nosed, common sense, unequivocal evidence for the existence of currently unaccepted assump-

tions is presented by those who have thoroughly attenuated their childish ends for particular beliefs, I hope I am
prepared to examine it and thoroughly. The pitfalls of
group interlock are quite as insidious as the pitfalls of
one's own fantasizing.

Group acceptance of undemonstrated existence theorems and of seductive beliefs adds no more validity to
the theorems and to the beliefs than our fantasizing can
add. Anaclitic group behavior is no better than
solitudinous fantasies of the truth. Where agreed-upon
truth can exist in the science of the innermost realities is
not and cannot yet be settled. Beginnings have been
made by many men, satisfying proofs by none—yet.

10

Basic Metaprograms of Existence

ELIEF EXPERIMENTS BRING UP several meta-theoretical considerations. At one extreme of the organization of human thinking is the formal logical basic assumption set of meta-theories. I conducted these experiments and interpreted the results from this point of view.

Preliminary to the experiments in changing basic beliefs, many experiments with the profound physical isolation and solitude—the void space—were carried out over a period of several years. These experiences were followed by combining the entheogenic state achieved with LSD-25 and the physical isolation state in a second period of several years. The minimum time between experiments was thirty days, the maximum time several months.

BELIEF EXPERIMENTS BRING UP several meta-theoretical considerations.

All of the following experiments were done looking upward in the functional organization of the biocomputer from the self-programmer to the supra-self-metaprograms. A converse set of experiments was done in which the self-metaprogrammer looked downward towards the metaprograms, the programs and the lower levels of the computer's organizational structure.

Bodily Operations Are Automatic

BODY AND BRAIN OPERATE without our paying any attention to it. When entering the isolation of the void space I have faith that I can consciously ignore the necessities of breathing and other bodily functions and that they will take care of themselves automatically without my detailed attention. This allows existence metaprograms to be made in relative safety.

In the profound physical isolation situation of the void space we acquire, or we have, or we develop a confidence in our body to function quite automatically and to take care of itself. The problem of air supply, keeping your face above the water, the action of respiration and of heart are all turned over to the protohuman survival programs to maintain themselves. All tendencies to control or to monitor respiration or heart action should be avoided. The same applies to the gastrointestinal tract and the genitourinary tract insofar as can be achieved automatic operations of these systems should be encouraged. As they gradually assume their proper low-level expression in our psychic life, confidence in the body's continued operation without attention by the self—the self-metaprogramer—can be achieved. These considerations are particularly important with the more powerful entheogens such as LSD-25 as the physical isolation and solitude begin to develop.

> All tendencies to control or to monitor respiration or heart action should be avoided.

I confirmed this axiom by successful leaving of my body and parking it in isolation for periods of twenty minutes to two hours in sixteen different experiments. This success, in turn, allowed other basic beliefs to be experimented upon. The basic belief that I could leave the body and explore new universes was successfully programmed in the first eight different experiments lasting from five minutes to forty minutes. The later eight experiments were on the cognitional multidimensional space without the leaving the body metaprogram.

Seek Those Beings Whom We Control and Who Exist in Us

WITH THIS PROGRAM I FOUND OLD MODELS IN MYSELF—old programs, old metaprograms—implanted by others, implanted by self, injected by parents, by teachers, and so forth. I found that these were disparate and separate autonomous beings in myself. I thought of them as a noisy group. My incorporated parents, my siblings, my offspring, my teachers, my wife seemed to be a disorganized crowd within me, each running and arguing a program with me and in me. While I watched, battles took place between these models. I settled many disparate and nonintegrated points between these beings and gradually incorporated more of them into the self-metaprogram.

After many weeks of self-analysis outside the void space, with some help from my former analyst, I saw that these beings within the self were also those other beings outside self of the other experiments. I thought of the projected as-if-outside beings as cognitional carnivores attempting to eat up my self-metaprogram and wrest control from me. As the various levels of metaprograms became straightened out, I was able to categorize and begin to control the various levels as they were presented during these experiments. As my apparently unconscious needs for credence in these beliefs were attenuated with analytic work, my freedom to move from one set of basic beliefs to another was increased and the anxiety associated with this kind of movement gradually disappeared.

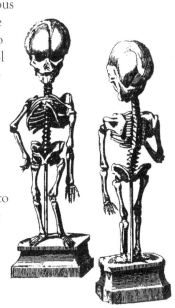

Other Beings Can Be Contacted

As I MASTERED BASIC NAVIGATIONAL SKILLS in this dimension, my next challenge was the metaprogram "other beings can be contacted" to seek beings other than myself, not human, in whom I existed and who control me and other human beings. I found whole new universes containing great varieties of beings, some greater than myself, some equal to myself, and some lesser than myself. I described my experiences during this exploration in my autobiography, *The Scientist.*

Beings greater than myself were a set so huge in space-time as to make me feel as a mere mote in their sunbeam, a single microflash of energy in their time scale. All my years are but an instant in their lifetime, a single thought in their vast computer, a mere particle in their assemblages of living cognitive units. I felt I was in the absolute unconscious of these beings. I experienced many more sets all so much greater than myself that they were almost inconçeivable in their complexity, size and time scales.

Good vs. Evil

THOSE BEINGS WHICH WERE CLOSE TO ME IN COMPLEXITY, size and time were dichotomized into the evil ones and the good ones. The evil ones were busy with purposes so foreign to my own that I had many near-misses and almost fatal accidents in encounters with them. They were almost totally unaware of my existence and hence almost wiped me out, apparently without knowing it. The good ones directed good thoughts to me, through me, and to one another. They were at least conceivably human and humane. I interpreted them as alien yet friendly. They were not so alien as to be completely removed from human beings in regard to their purposes and activities, however.

Some of these beings are programmed for the long term. They nurture us. They experiment on us. They control the probability of our discovering and exploiting new science. Discoveries such as nuclear energy, LSD, RNA-DNA, as examples, are under probability control by these beings. Further, humans are tested by some of these beings and cared for by others. Some of them have programs which include survival and progress. Others have programs which include opposition to these good programs and include our ultimate demise as a species. The evil ones are willing to sacrifice us in their experiments. Hence they are alien and removed from us. Only limited choices are still available to us as a species. We are an ant colony in their laboratory.

Controlling Beings

IN ANOTHER SET OF EXPERIMENTS—explorations, I employed the metaprogram, "controlling beings exist." I assumed the existence of beings in whom humans exist and who directly control humans. This is a tighter control than the previous one and assumes continuous day and night, second to second control, as if each human being were a in a larger organism. Such beings insist upon activities in human being totally under the control of the organism of which each human being is a part. In this state there is no freedom for an individual. I entered this supra-self-metaprogram twice. Each time I had to leave it because it was too anxiety-provoking. In the first case I became part of a vast computer in which I was one element. In the second case I was a thought in a much larger mind and was being modified rapidly, flexibly and plastically.

A basic overall metaprogram was finally generated. For my intellectual satisfaction I found that I best assume that all of the phenomena that took place existed only in my own brain and in my own mind. Other assumptions about the existence of these beings are suitable subjects for research rather than subjects for blind—unconscious, conscious—belief for me.

Space-Time Explorations

I EXPERIMENTED WITH MOVEMENTS OF SELF forward and back in space-time. When attempting to go forward into the future I began to realize my goals for that future and imagine wishful thinking solutions to current problems. When I put in the metaprogram for going back into my own childhood, real and fantasy memories were evoked and integrated. When I pushed back through to the *in utero* situation, I found an early nightmare which was reinvoked and solved. Relying on my scientific knowledge, I pushed the program back through previous generations— prehuman primates, carnivores, fish and protozoa—to experience a sperm-egg explosion on the way through this past reinvocation of imaginary experience.

The last set of experiments was made possible by the results of the previous set. Progress in controlling the projection metaprogram resulted from the other universes experiments. Finally I understood and became familiar with my need for fantasized other universes.

Analytic work allowed me to bypass this need and penetrate into the cognitional multidimensional projection spaces. Experiments in programming in this innermost space showed results quite satisfying to a high degree of credence in the belief that experiments in the series showed inner happenings without heeding the participation of outer causes. The need for the constant use of outer causes was found to be a projected outward metaprogram to avoid taking personal responsibility for portions of the contents of my own mind. My dislike for certain kinds of my nonsensical programs caused me to project them and thus avoid admitting they were mine.

Critical Skepticism

IN SUMMATION, the subjectively apparent results of the experiments were to straighten out a good deal of the "nonsense" in my biocomputer. Through these experiments I was able to examine some warded-off beliefs and defensive structures accumulated throughout my life. The net result was a feeling of greater integration of self and a feeling of positive affect for the current structure of myself, combined with an improved skepticism of the validity of subjective judging of events in self.

Some objective testing of these essentially subjective judgments have been initiated through cooperation with other persons. Such objective testing is very difficult. This area needs a great deal of future research work. We need better investigative techniques, combining subjective and behavioral—verbal—techniques. The major feeling that I had after such experiences and experiments is that the fluidity and plasticity of my biocomputer has certain limits to it, and that those limits have been enlarged somewhat by the experiments. How long such enlargement lasts and to what extent are still not known of course. A certain amount of continued critical skepticism about and in the self-metaprogram—and in its felt changes—is very necessary for a scientist exploring these areas.

11

Personal Metaprogram Language

F THE LANGUAGES POSSESSED by one's self some are used to control the metaprogrammatic level as seen in the functional organization of the biocomputer on page 68. The self-metaprogrammer exerts control through the personal metaprogrammatic language. This is the language which controls the biocomputer itself, how it operates, and how it computes as an integral whole. Each human biocomputer has a unique private control language in its unique stored programs, stored metaprograms, and stored self-metaprograms. Cognitive psychologists call it "self-talk." This language is not shared in the usual public domain of the language acquired in childhood.

This control language and control of the biocomputer itself can be changed as new understanding of control allows new control. This language has aspects which are nonverbal, nonvocal and can be more emotional and mathematical than they are linguistic. Here we are expressing some linguistic aspects and some of the mathematical nonverbal experiences. We are limited in public expression of these experiences to the consensus non-private language.

The experiments were designed along the lines of finding solutions to certain personal problems within the biocomputer. These problems are the basic ones of the presence of antithetical and contradictory metaprograms.

Looking again at the functional organization, some of these paradoxical and agonistic problems appear at the supra-self-metaprogram level and some at the metaprogram level. One such experiment was on a spontaneous occurrence of a phrase, during an entheogenic state, which took on elements of humor and the aspect as if of a great discovery. The private metaprogrammatic control instruction WAS *The key is no key.*

The Key Is No Key

IN THE EXTERNAL REALITY, stimulus for this statement was a number of keys which I had been carrying around for several years. I suddenly became aware that I had in my life many locks. Thus it was necessary for me to carry many keys. At times these keys were felt as a physical and a mental burden which slowed the efficient operation of my life. These were aspects of the phrase key which were real keys, real locks on real doors to real rooms, real houses, real offices, and so forth. At that particular moment this seemed to be the epitome of modern civilization—to have doors, to have locks on those doors, and have privileged persons who possessed the keys to open those doors.

I next moved from the meanings in the external reality metaprogram to another level in which I internalized this picture of the door, the room, the lock, the key. I visualized my antithetical metaprograms as existing in rooms separated by doors which had locks on them. I was searching for the keys to open the doors.

As these inner rooms—categories, problems, antitheses—became embodied in the locked door imagined-projected metaphor I began to walk through metaprogrammatic storage looking for a key to open the next door into the further recesses of the rooms. As I moved I began to see that the doors were defined as doors by my biocomputer. Similarly my computer defined locks as locks and keys were defined as necessary to open the locks.

In a moment of insight, I saw that the defined boundaries—the doors, the walls, ceilings, the floors, and the locks themselves and their keys—were a convenient metaprogram dividing up my knowledge and my control mechanisms into compartments in an artificial personal fashion.

I explored many rooms with many different kinds of knowledge in the rooms. The walls slowly began to dissolve, some of them melted and flowed away. Other rooms were revealed as solid and the doors with secure locks rather numerous. Some keys were missing.

Most of the hypothesized building inside my mind now became open spaces with information freely available without the former walls between arbitrary rooms of categories. Those rooms, locks, and keys that were left were quite basic to the development of my self-metaprogram.

Some of these rooms were created in childhood in response to situations over which the self-metaprogrammer had no control. These rooms housed ideas and systems of thinking which evoked intense fear or intense anger as I approached with the intent of opening the doors. The locks did not respond to frontal assaults. These rooms turned out to be very difficult to define out of existence in order to have their contents interact with the rest of the metaprogrammatic level.

I underwent a frantic and frightened search for the keys to the locks of these strong-rooms. I became alternately fearful and angry. I made several assaults on walls, doors, ceilings and floors of these closed rooms without much success. I went away from these rooms into other universes and other spaces and left my biocomputer to work out solutions below my levels of awareness.

Later with higher motivational energy I returned to problem of the locks, the doors and the rooms somewhat refreshed by the experiences in the other realms. Mathematical transformations were next tried in approaching the locked rooms. The concept of the key fitting into the lock and the necessity of finding the key were abandoned and the rooms were approached as topological puzzles. In the multidimensional cognitional and visual space the rooms were now manipulated without the necessity of the key in the lock.

Topological Transformation

USING THE TRANSITIONAL CONCEPT that the lock is a hole in the door through which we can exert an effort for a topological transformation, we could turn the room into another topological form other than a closed box. The room in effect was turned inside out through the hole, through the lock leaving the contents outside and the room now a collapsed balloon placed farther from the self-metaprogrammer. Room after room was thus defined as turned inside out with the contents spewed forth for use by the self-metaprogrammer. Once this control key worked, it continued automatically to its own limits.

With this sort of an "intellectual crutch," entire new areas of basic beliefs were entered upon. Most of the rooms, which before had appeared as strong rooms with big powerful walls, doors, and locks, now ended up as empty balloons. The greatly defended contents of the rooms in many cases turned out to be relatively trivial programs and episodes from childhood, which had been over-generalized and overvalued by my biocomputer. The devaluation of the general purpose properties of the human biocomputer was one such room. In childhood the many episodes which led to the self-metaprogrammer not remaining general purpose but becoming more and more limited and specialized were entered upon. Several layers of the supra-self-metaprograms laid down in child-hood were opened up.

The mathematical operation which took place in the computer was the movement of energies and masses of data from the supra-self-metaprogram down to the self-metaprogrammatic level and below. At the same time there was the knowledge that programmatic materials had been moved from the supra-self-position to the under-self-controlled position at the programmatic level. These operations were all filed in metaprogram storage under the title, "The key is no key."

External Reality

THE NECESSITY FOR LOCKS and for keys in the real world had to be dealt with. There was an interval of time in which I was quite willing to throw all of my keys away and keep all of the real doors of my life unlocked. That was tried briefly and resulted in a theft. This immediately brought home the obvious fact that the external reality programs cannot be controlled by the self-metaprogram. There are other human biocomputers and a real external reality, which has unpredictable properties not under the control of the self-metaprogrammer. Therefore there must remain in the supra-self-metaprogram certain rules for conduct of the human computer in the external reality. There must remain a certain modicum of real supra-self control and respect for the external reality's part of the supra-self-metaprogram.

> The province of the mind is the only area of science in which what one believes to be true either is true or becomes true.

The province of the mind is the only area of science in which what one believes to be true either is true or becomes true within limits to be determined experimentally. I saw that the key is no key is a private self-metaprogramming language phrase and should not be applied to the external reality metaprogram nor should it be applied to other human biocomputers—at least not without careful consideration of their capabilities and their own supra-self-metaprograms. Similar topological transformations under control of the self-metaprogrammer may not yet have developed within the given other person. The kinds of phenomena expressed by this unique private human biocomputer—The key is no key—may be totally inapplicable to others.

Meta-theoretically considered, however, the above operation can be re-expressed by a given individual and elaborated and differentiated along other coordinates. For those willing to try these experiments I wish to add a suggestion. It is necessary to explore all aspects of your body image, your childish emotional regions, your real body in various states and with special stimuli in addition to those from the body itself. With such explorative training you can do topological transformations which can result in step-wise changes in metaprogramming and in metaprograms themselves. Bias, prejudice, preconception and intransigence in explicit areas are seen as supra-self-metaprograms which are inappropriate. Until there can be highly motivated mathematical transformations within the areas of control metaprograms, major changes are not made.

Linguistic Symbols

THE ABOVE ALL-TOO-CONDENSED SUMMARY of these experiments and their results illustrates the linguistic symbolization of mathematical operations. This operation offers a kind of shorthand to the human biocomputer. Linguistic symbols can be used for storing instructions which represent whole areas of operations in the computer. The key is no key is a version of the actual operations which it symbolizes. The statement is in the language of the child as the young computer originally stored it. The actual operations taking place in the adult symbolized by the key is no key are a complex rendering of more advanced ideas, some of which are circuit-like, some of which are topological transformations and some of which are in multidimensional matrices.

A given human computer is limited in its operations by its own acquired mathematical conceptual machinery—this is part of its supra-self-metaprograms. Maximum control over the metaprogrammatic level by the self-metaprogram is achieved not by direct "one to one" orders and instructions from the one level to the other.

The control is based upon exploration of n-dimensional spaces and finding key points for transformations, first in decisive small local regions, which can result in large-scale transformations. This modeling brings to mind Ashby's *Design for a Brain*, in which a large "homeostat" stimulated in one small region makes large adjustments throughout itself in order to compensate for the small change.

One key in the mind is to hunt for those discontinuities in the structure of the thinking, which reveal a critical turnover point at which we can exert emotional energy so as to cause a transformation in all of that region.

The analogy of the key in the lock is part of my biocomputer as a child. The lock is now transformed into an n-dimensional choice-point at which I could exert the proper amount of energy in the proper dimensions and in proper directions in those dimensions and find a radical transformation of all the metaprograms in that region of the computer.

In a three-dimensional geometrical model of such operations, in which I decrease the number of dimensions so that they can be visualized in visual space, I can think of oddly-shaped rubber surfaces connected on lines, on points and over large areas which are inflated to different amounts and differing pressures so as to fill a very large room. These membranes are of different colors and various regions are differently lighted and the whole is considered to be pulsing and changing shapes but not hanging contact between surfaces, lines, or points. I imagined myself moving through these complex surfaces. There are various colors lighted from various directions. I hunted for that zone in which I could exert maximum amount of effect in terms of the redistribution of bond energies, over point, line, and surface areas of contact. I could also exert the maximum effect on the differential pressures in the spaces bounded by each of the surfaces where closed.

Fluid

AFTER SUFFICIENT STUDY OF THIS MODEL I discovered that the points of contact between the membranes are not as fixed as when first seen. What I saw at first was a frozen instant of time extending over a long period of time as if the model were static. Suddenly I realized that the points of contact are the sharing of portions of these surfaces along appropriate lines at given instants and that these boundaries are changing constantly. I suddenly also discovered that the colors were moving over the surfaces and passing the boundaries. This particular model is a small region in a larger universe filled with such surfaces and intersections and spaces between. I discovered that the light sources are within certain of these sheets shining through to others and that the hue and intensity are varying according to some local rules.

I moved away from the model and saw that it is filling a universe. I moved back into the model and began to look carefully at one thin membrane. As the structure of the membrane was revealed and I saw the structure of the intersection within membranes. There was microcircuitry within the membrane at a molecular and atomic level. There were energies moving in prescribed paths—sometimes in a noisy fashion—in multiple directions within the membrane. At the intersections collisions occur—electrons, mesons, protons, neutrons, neutrinos, and so forth were moving from one sheet to the other in both directions. Sheets that were immediately adjacent were doing local computations at very high speed. I saw the intersections as micromolecular-atomic switch lines, switch surfaces, and switch points.

Thus I found that the phrase "The key is no key" had grown into a new conception of a biocomputer. My biocomputer within itself ideally recognizes no locks, no forbidden transitions, no areas in which data cannot be freely moved from one zone to another. At the boundaries of the biocomputer, however, there were still categorical imperatives. The problem became not the boundaries within the computer but the boundaries outside it. By outside I do not mean only the integumentary boundaries of the real body, but also other sources of influence through the bottom layer of the external chemical physical reality.

To symbolize this doubt, this skepticism, about the boundaries of the biocomputer and the influences that can be brought to bear upon them other than those coming through the physical-chemical reality, a line is placed above the supra-self-metaprograms and is labeled unknown. In my mind, the unknown must take precedence. It is placed above the supra-self-metaprogram because it contains some of the goals of the human biocomputer.

Worth Exploring

EXPLORATION OF THE INNER REALITY presupposes that the inner reality contains large unknowns which are worth exploring. To explore them it is necessary to recognize their existence and to prepare our computer for the exploration. If we are to explore the unknown we should take the minimum amount of baggage and not load our self down with conceptual machinery which cannot be flexibly reoriented to accept and investigate the unknown. The next stage of development of those who have the courage and the necessary inner apparatus to do it, is exploration in depth of this vast inner unknown region. For this task we need the best kind of thinking of which we are capable. We must dissolve and/or reprogram the doctrinaire ideological approaches to these questions.

> In my mind, the unknown must take precedence

Remain Skeptical

IT IS DESIRABLE TO REMAIN SKEPTICAL of this approach to this region. We must not overvalue this particular approach, but instead always look for alterative approaches for exploratory purposes. Freedom from the tyranny of the supra-self-metaprograms must be sought but not to the point at which other human biocomputers control our biocomputer. Deep and basic interlock between selected human biocomputers is needed for this exploration. Conceptualization of the thinking machine itself is needed by the best minds available for this task. In a sense, we create the explorers in this area.

12

Programming
Chemicals

ERTAIN CHEMICAL SUBSTANCES have programmatic and metaprogrammatic effects. That is, they change the operations of the biocomputer at the programmatic level and at the metaprogrammatic level. Substances of interest at the metaprogrammatic level are those that allow reprogramming and those that facilitate modifications of metaprograms. The positive pleasure-producing and negative pain or fear-producing aspects of the programs and metaprograms strike at the very roots of motivational energies for the biocomputer. One aspect of many entheogens is that they can give an overall positive motivational aspect to the individual in the altered state. This may facilitate program modifications, but it also can facilitate seeking pleasure as a goal of itself.

Commonly used terms for these substances are loaded with diagnostic, therapeutic, medical, moral, ethical, and legal connotations. To be scientifically useful the social connotations must be removed. I use terms like "psychopharmacologically active drugs," "psychotomimetics," "tranquilizers," "narcotics," "drugs," "anesthetics," "analgesics," and "entheogens" without the therapeutic, diagnostic, moral, ethical, and legal connotations. The term "reprogramming substances" may be appropriate for compounds like lysergic acid diethylamide (LSD) and entheogenic plants like peyote and psilocybin mushrooms. For substances like ethyl alcohol—alcohol, liquor, beer—the term "metaprogram-attenuating substances" is useful.

Entheogens

USE OF THE ENTHEOGENIC AGENTS, such as ayahausca, peyote, and LSD, can change the biocomputer's operations in certain ways. Entheogen means bring out the god within. Such chemical substances instruct self-metaprograms to create special states. Many of these special states have been described in the literature on hypnosis.

The powerful entheogenic agent lysergic acid diethylamide (LSD-25) has been shown by many investigators to cause large changes in the modes of functioning of the human biocomputer. The dosage to obtain various effects ranges from 25 to 1000 micrograms per subject per session. The detectable primary effects have a time course, a latency of 20-40 minutes, from time of administration and endure for 4 to 12 hours for single or divided doses, with a peak effect at 2 to 3 hours. At the same dose level, such effects cannot be repeated for 72 to 144 hours. Detectable secondary and tertiary effects have a longer time course. With sufficiently sensitive testing techniques, secondary effects with half-life of 1 to 6 weeks have been described. Tertiary effects can be detected for 1 to 2 years.

The descriptions in the literature of the primary effects vary considerably. The frameworks of these descriptions show a great variety of phenomenological, philosophical, medical, psychiatric, psychological, social and religious conceptualizations. Published mechanisms and models of the phenomena are found to be unsatisfactory. Published experiments resulting from the use of these models are also not satisfactory.

As a result of this dissatisfaction with published materials, a new model was constructed—the human biocomputer. Interactive experiments were designed to test this model with entheogenic sessions. Subjects were preprogrammed with the general concepts of the model over several months before the first session, and with specific programs to be tested 12 hours to one hour before each session. During separate sessions (LSD dose range of 100-400 micrograms), programming was done (a) by subject, (b) written instructions, (c) taped instructions, (d) environmental control and (e) one other person. Results were dictated during some sessions or transcribed immediately after each session. Follow-up analyses were similarly recorded for periods up to several months.

Modifications of the model were made as the necessity arose during the long-term analyses, and introduced in each later session as specific instructions. The model is one that continues to evolve in a general purpose and open-ended a way as is possible for this investigator.

This account gives a report of the current state of this model of the human biocomputer, some of the properties found, the programming and metaprogramming done, the concepts evolved, the special isolation-solitude environment, and special metaprogramming techniques developed.

Self-Metaprogramming With Entheogens

A SERIES OF EXPERIMENTS WERE DESIGNED and carried out in the entheogenic state in the physical isolation, and solitude of the void space to test the validity of the basic assumptions implicit in the theory of the human biocomputer. One point of primary interest during these experiments was to find out what level of intensity of belief in a set of assumptions could be achieved. The assumptions tested in this set of experiments are not those of current science. They are not in the conscious working repertory of myself as a scientist, nor were they consciously acceptable to me.

It is not my intention to give all of the details of either the self-metaprogramming language that was used or the details of the elicited phenomena. The account, which is purposely sparse, condensed, and compressed, is abstracted from the complexity of the totality of the experiments includes only those formal descriptions which may serve as guide posts to others attempting to reproduce these or similar experiments. It is not intended to complicate this account with the personal aspects of the metaprogramming, the elicited phenomena, or difficulties encountered. For those researchers who are interested in this work's reproduction in themselves, these assumptions and these results can be translated into their own metaprogramming language and such workers can obtain their unique results. There are a number of experimenters with entheogenic states who write as if they believe implicitly in the objective reality of causes outside themselves for certain kinds of experiences undergone with these particular beliefs. I do not claim validity of details beyond myself. There probably are those explorers who are prepared well enough to attempt reproducing what has been done here in themselves. This particular set of existence theorems was selected for experiment for a number of reasons.

Data Storage Systems

ENTHEOGENS FACILITATE entering into the data storage systems. Taboo or forbidden programs are not fully constructed. There are peculiar gaps indicating forbidden areas. Within realizable limits most other programs can be produced. The way the material is held in the dynamic storage is entirely strange to the conscious self. You can produce displays of data patterns, of instructions, of data storage contents, or of current problems. A *display* is any visual, or acoustic, or tactile, olfactory or taste plotting of a set of discriminative variables in any

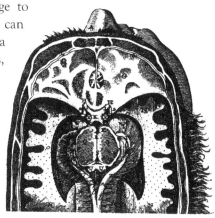

number of dimensions of the currently available materials. The motivational sign and intensity can be varied in any of these displays under special orders.

More or less complete replays of past experiences important in current computations can be programmed from data storage. Objective time relative to original occurrence is not an important aspect of the filing system. Of greater import is the level of maturation of the biocomputer at the time of the initial occurrence of the experience.

Emotional Intensity

STORED OCCURRENCES, INSTRUCTIONS AND PROGRAMS vary in the amount and specificity of the positive and negative emotions attached to each. If too negative—evil, harmful, fearful, traumatic—an emotional charge is attached. This can become what people often call a "button" as in "you pushed my button". Replay can allow readjustment toward the positive end of the motivation-feeling-emotion spectrum. When in an intense entheogenic state, the negative or the positive charge can be changed to neutral or to its opposite by special instructions. However, since most people wish to avoid the negative and encourage the positive once they obtain control over programming they tend to put a positive charge on stored occurrences, on the programs and metaprograms and the processes of creating them. A chemical change may take place in signal storage as the sign of the motivational process shifts from negative to positive.

The instructions are carried out generally in minutes. Of course, the time varies with the complexity of the task being programmed into the biocomputer. Previous experience with using entheogens to self-programming is important. The more often you have done so, the easier it is to do again and the less time it takes.

This level of manipulation and control of our programs, and its rather dramatic presentation to our self, is difficult to achieve without the use of entheogens. This amount of control resembles other ways of achieving control and visual projection but in actual intensity I know of no other way to achieve it, with the possible exception of hypnosis or the deep meditation of an advanced adept.

Growth Hypothesis

ONE MAJOR BIOLOGICAL EFFECT OF POWERFUL ENTHEOGENS may be a selective effect on growth patterns in the CNS. Some parts of the CNS are thought to be specifically accelerated in their local growth patterns, such as the systems which are selectively active during the entheogenic state.

Kinds of Central States

(0) Sleeping

(1) Neutral

(2) Activated

(3) Inhibited

(4) Rewarding

(5) Punishing

(6) Disinhibited

(7) Integrative

(8) Ambivalent

For these postulated growth effects there is an optimal concentration of the substance in the brain. With less concentration than the optimal there is merely an irritating stimulation of the CNS which is below the levels of awareness. At the optimal concentration, in the non-tolerant state, the phenomena of the entheogenic state occur. This is a phase of initiation of new growth in the CNS. This phase is a state of mind analogous to that presumed to exist in the very young human, possibly beginning in the fetus or embryo.

If additional material is administered, prolongation of this phase can be achieved within certain limits. With the maintenance of the optimal concentration of entheogenic substance, this phase is prolonged by hours until tolerance develops. The phase of developed tolerance is thought to be the phase of the completion of the fast new growth. Most of the new biochemical and neurological connections are completed.

Places in CNS for Central States

(0) Sleep system

(1) Afferent projective systems

(2) Efferent projection systems

(3) Primary activation systems

(4) Primary inhibition systems

(5) Reward systems

(6) Punishment systems

(7) Integration systems

(8) Pattern storage systems

(9) Programming systems

If continuous maintenance of optimal concentration for many hours after this initial phase is then achieved, growth may continue slowly. The growth is not thought to be confined to the central nervous system. The autonomic nervous system may grow also. If the optimal concentration is exceeded, the entheogenic substance excites a "stress syndrome" stimulating the adrenal-vascular-gastro intestinal tract. This response is separate from the affective results of the entheogenic state which can cause a stress syndrome in certain individuals. I am not speaking of such individuals. I am speaking of more sophisticated explorers who have been through the necessary and sufficient experiences to be able avoid a stress syndrome in the entheogenic state.

At concentrations above the optimal there can be a reversal of the beneficial effects in the induced stress syndrome so that anti-growth factors are stimulated. Homeostasis is thus assured in the organism. A similar phenomenon can be seen with negative programming during an intense entheogenic experience. Reversal of growth may be programmed in by the self-programmer, unconscious metaprograms, or by an outside therapist or other persons.

Feedback Causes in Central States

1. Patterns of immediate results of outside stimuli (strength, place, timing).

2. Patterns of immediate results of responses.

3. Stored integrated consequences patterns.

4. Continuous current cortical integration of selected past stored patterns and current results of outside stimuli and responses.

5. Cellular biochemical states of storage-depletion of specific substances in specific sites: reserves available in body.

6. Specific CNS biochemical states locally.

7. Built-in programs.

At concentrations above optimal the resulting stress syndrome is programmed into the autonomic nervous system and continues beyond the time of the presence of the substance to repeat itself until reprogrammed out days or weeks later. At levels above optimal, the self-

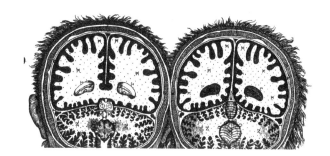

metaprogram loses energy and circularity to autonomous programs. At very high levels the ego disappears.

This complex series of relations shows the delicate nature of the best state for re-metaprogramming and of re-metaprogramming itself. Until sophisticated handling of these substances can be achieved, careful voluntary education of professional personnel should be done—and done carefully with insight. Selection of persons for training must be diplomatic and tactful—carried out cooperatively without publicity. Candor and honesty at deep levels is a prime requisite.

13
Training
Sessions

S A PRAGMATIC MATTER the explorer should do self-analysis in the severely attenuated physical reality—the void space or solitude—without use of any entheogen for several exposures before using the substance. You must learn not only to tolerate but to *like* the solitude experience for several hours at a time. Fears of the unreleased unconscious programming can be attenuated and analyzed during this period.

Training sessions with an entheogen such as LSD-25 with another person must be done before it is combined with the profound physical isolation and solitude. During this period, training by the external screens and the projections can be done. During this period the explorer must face the fears of the entheogenic substance itself and the fears of damage to the brain and the mind by this agent. The explorer must also face the hedonistic, narcissistic pleasure induction and maintenance possible with entheogens, and must make a decision about how to handle these pleasures versus those which are brought about in the external reality.

Reprogramming Mistakes

THERE IS AN ADDITIONAL CAUTION in the use of entheogens in self-metaprogramming. The self-programmer must be strong enough to experience these phenomena and not make difficult-to-reverse mistakes in reprogramming or difficult-to-correct errors in new commitments in the external world. Employing entheogens as a reprogramming catalyst is only for the most experienced and strongest personalities—with the right training. I strongly caution that these methods be used only under very controlled and studied conditions with as near ideal as possible physical and social environment and help from thoroughly trained empathic-matching persons. The self-programmer's short-term and long-term welfare must unconsciously and consciously control all actions, all speech, and all transactions between each pair of persons present.

Choice of Attending Persons

IT MUST BE UNDERSCORED THAT ANY ACTION, facial appearance, word, sentence, tone of voice, or gesture on the part of the attending person can be used by a person in the entheogenic state in the processes of penetration, elicitation, or reprogramming. Mistakes by the attending person can have devastating power and must be scrupulously avoided. Only mature, experienced, previously-exposed persons should be allowed in the external reality during this critical time. One attending person is best. Ideally this one attending person should have been psychoanalyzed and have pursued self-analysis with entheogenic aid as well as in the physical isolation and solitude of the void space. Short of this ideal, high quality professional psychoanalytic training is a minimum ideal requirement. Lacking that, then the attending person should be careful selected by such professionals.

> Only mature, experienced, previously-exposed persons should be allowed in the external reality during this critical time.

Exclusion test

AN EXCLUSION TEST MUST BE DONE on potential attendants and therapists. They should have been personally through several powerful entheogenic sessions themselves with the self-analysis metaprograms as the leading motivating instructions, and have penetrated to and beyond their own buried lethality and hostility. The professional selector should be thoroughly acquainted with the potential aides, and evaluate the stages through which they have passed and achieved "permanently."

There can be special cases, less than the above ideal, but consonant with the principles enunciated. Some spouses or lovers have special understanding and inter-locks which allow certain kinds of deep penetrations, elicitations and reprogrammings, but not other kinds. If one of the pair has been through entheogenic-facilitated self-analysis training, it is possible in special cases for that person to help the other member through a session by being a standby monitor and positive love-object in the external reality. However, there should be some form of professional psychoanalytic control over such sessions. Controls can vary from being implicit and in the nature of tactical and strategic advisory sessions to being external realty supervisory, depending on the ego strength and on the current stage of development of each member of the pair. Expert and informed clinical judgment after thor-ough clinical study is the best instrument for such deci-sions.

Repetitive Unconscious Replay

CERTAIN KINDS OF PROGRAMS in the human computer are circular and usually below the ordinary levels of aware-ness. Circularity can be useful and needed or misused, such as in the maintenance of desperate and disturbing programs. A program in a certain patient says, "Mommy has abandoned baby, run to Daddy. Daddy beats me and leaves. Mommy comforts me and leaves. Daddy loves me and hurts me and leaves. Run to Mommy. Mommy has my sister, loves her, abandons me. Run to Daddy. Daddy hurts. Daddy leaves. Run to Mommy. Mommy leaves . . . Mommy has abandoned baby." Again and again the program cycles. When the patient was a baby this was an important reality program. It became a fixed circular reality program and carried into adulthood.

Repetitive replay programs operate slowly or rapidly—
and continuously. In the adult, the real situation in the
external reality can not halt the circular program. Usually
modeling in the reality is preeminent over such circularity,
but in the circular case, external reality is used to facilitate playback and maintain the strength of the old model
program. Any important man or woman in the external
reality must—somehow—be made to fit into this "ancient
model" program. An external observer sees a person with
such a program repeating an unhappy pattern again and
again over the years. The underlying perpetuated baby
program is unavailable for inspection, replay and breaking
of circularity by the owner as an adult.

At high doses, powerful entheogens like LSD-25 can
reduce the relative strength of the external program by
enhancing the strength of other programs. With LSD-25
this occurs with 200 to 400 micrograms, starts in the
first hour and can continue for four or more hours.
Entheogens can increase the strength of and activate
basic models in storage. They also allow for the imple-
mentation of self-metaprogramming orders—orders stored
just before the entheogen's maximum effect starts. If
present, strong circular programs are likely to be replayed.
The self-observer participates in the replay and is programmed again but this reprogramming of the replay
program is relatively weak as compared to the time of the
implanting episodes in the external reality when the
person was as a baby or child. The self-observer sees a
dramatic, repeat performance of new replays—again and
again,.

Each replay is slightly different and gives the outside
observer the feeling of a circular course not quite exactly
repeating each time. The emotion expressed at first has
all the desperate panic of the child. However, gradually
the spectrum of intense emotion can be experienced and
expressed progressively. With proper external reality personnel, and responses from them, progress leads the circle
gradually out of negative feelings into the regions of good

feelings so that fear and other negative emotions are extinguished. Good feelings are attached to replay and the self finally can see it operate with its new emotion and— possibly for the first time—examine its newly charged positive structure as it replays and reduces its importance on the unconscious priority list so that it can be filed as a relic of childhood in the inoperative or weakly operating "history" file.

Increased Energy

FOR A TIME, THE SELF FEELS FREE—CLEANED OUT. The strength gained can be immense. The energy freed is double because the fight with the circular program is temporarily gone. For a short time, energy taken from the old circular program and the energy formerly expended in the fight may be available. Not only is the energy of self no longer absorbed in the fight, but new program energy is available. So twice the energy of the circular program can be made available for use by the self-metaprogram in constructing new energy relations between desired programs directed toward ideals, aims, and goals. Adult love and sharing consonant with aspirations and external reality gain strength and gain differentiation of response and of interlocks. Humor appears in abundance—good humor. Beauty is enhanced. Bodily appearance becomes youthful, with increased smiles and good-natured puns and jokings at a deep level of understanding and perspective. The babyish and the childish aspects of self are converted to adulthood with great strength of character, integrity, and loving. These positive effects can last as long as two to four weeks before re-assertion of the old program takes place.

Survival Programs

Some programs carry the ability to lead the way into potentially destructive action or even to destroy the individual biocomputer. A metaprogram to neutralize programs with self-destruction in them is necessary. The use of powerful entheogens like LSD-25 in self-analysis allows quick penetration to such buried lethality.

Caution

A DEFINITE CAUTION IS ADVISED in the use of this technique. Until such destructive unconscious programs are found, thoroughly investigated, and understood in terms of the metaprogrammatic future, professional supervision is recommended. Such supervision should oversee the whole period of investigation and in detail, including before, during, and after a session for at least several days. It may be necessary that some of the instinctual patterns of behavior stirred up in the process of the session be acted-out in order to be tested, understood and filed properly in the metaprograms for the future plans of the individual. In this phase, dangers to self arise.

Protohuman Programs

THE STATES OF REVELATION of the implanted deeper programs may involve stages of childhood plus those presumed to have led Homo sapien, as an evolving primate, to civilization itself, and finally those leading into Mankind's own future beyond present accomplishment. Protohuman survival programs may appear near the beginning of the enthogenic-facilitated analyses, and sometimes later as well.

Protohuman programs include expressions of strong sexuality, gluttony, panic, anger, overwhelming guilt, sadomasochistic actions, fantasies, and superstitions. These programs have amazing strength and power over the self-metaprogrammer. Much of protohuman programs are wordless—existing in the emotion-feeling-motivational storage parts of the biocomputer. Protohuman programs usually have only poor representations in the modeling, clear thinking and verbal areas of the computer. Entheogens, and LSD-25 in particular, allow breakdown of the barriers between the wordless emotional systems and the word-filled modeling systems by means of channeled uninhibited feeling and channeled uninhibited action.

Danger sometimes lies in the unconscious being made conscious too rapidly. It is easy for the self-metaprogrammer to be overwhelmed by protohuman survival programs. When strong enough, the modeling systems of the self-metaprogrammer can receive the powerful currents of emotion in full force, go along with them, and eventually construct a vigorous operating model consonant with the desired ideal metaprograms—with built-in emotional power.

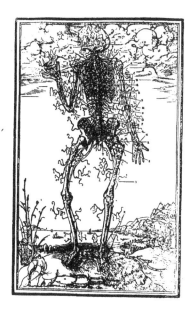

Death Wishes

ON THE ANALYTIC SIDE you must have analyzed and dealt with your unconscious death wishes. Up to a certain critical point we know and feel the probability of survival under conditions over which we have control. We have experienced internal mechanisms which may have tried to take over and deal a death-seeking blow to oneself. This kind of material must have been thoroughly analyzed with an external analyst before you approach experiments such as those discussed here. Your self and your analyst must be content that the level of control of such internal mechanisms is such that the probability of their dealing a death-seeking blow is low enough to risk exposure to these new conditions. This point cannot be emphasized strongly enough.

Those who are acquainted with the phenomena during classical psychoanalysis realize that certain kinds of personalities and certain individuals during analysis and after analysis can go through depressive phases in which such death wishes can be acted out. The seeds of destruction of self can be buried in the deeper metaprograms and programs of our biocomputer. Certain kinds of neuronal activities can destroy an organism. We must know of and be aware of the signs and the symbols of evocation of such death systems within our self.

Such negative phenomena are usually seen after the first or second session or two with a powerful entheogen. The residual unanalyzed portion of these programs are usually projected and acted out as a consequence of their release by the entheogenic agent. Several analytic sessions with an external analyst are necessary for maximum safety and minimum risk in these experiments.

In the farthest and deepest void state of isolation, basic needs and assumptions about self become evident. The existence of self and belief in the existence of self are made manifest. The positive or negative sign of values that we place upon self and upon the existence of self begins to show its force and strength. The problems discussed, but generally unfaced in a religious context in the external real world, are faced and can be lived out with a freedom unavailable since childhood.

Narcissistic States

Basic factors through electrical stimulation of the brain, drugs, programming, and isolation.

1. Prolonged hyperactive (+) systems.

2. Hypoactivity (-) systems.

3. Attenuation of external stimuli, responses, transactions.

Dissolution of Self

THE PROBLEM OF THE DISSOLUTION OF CONSCIOUS SELF by death of the body is studiable. Your evasions of this problem and of facing it can be projected into studiable areas of your experience. The existence theorem for spiritual and psychic entities is also testable and the strength of belief in these entities can be analyzed. Evasions of self-analysis and evasions of taking on certain beliefs can be tested.

In this area the denial and negation mechanisms of classical psychoanalysis show their strength. Previous analysis can train us to recognize that when data cannot be called up or when displays cannot be constructed or when certain operations cannot be carried out, we can see the cause currently existing. The set of inhibitory and repressive devices in our biocomputer is hard at work. In such inhibitory and repressive states preprogrammed sets of basic assumptions to be explored are incompletely carried out. We quickly find areas of the consequences of the assumed beliefs, which we cannot enter—only enter with fear, with anger, or with love—carried over from some other programming.

14
Projection Principles

N THE ANALYSIS OF THE EFFECTS of powerful entheogens like LSD-25 on the human mind, a reasonable hypothesis states that the effect of these substances on the human computer is to introduce white noise—in the sense of randomly varying energy containing no signals of itself—in specific systems in the computer. These systems and the partition of the noise among them vary with concentration of substance and with the substance used.

We can thus "explain" the apparent speedup of subjective time; the enhancement of colors and detail in perceptions of the real world; the production of illusions; the freedom to make new programs; the appearance of visual projections onto mirror images of the real face and body; the projections and apparent depth in colored and in black-and-white photos; the projection of emotional expression onto other real persons; the synesthesia of music to visual projections; the feeling of "oneness with the universe;" apparent ESP effects; communications from "beings other than humans;" the lowered close-analysis scores by outside scorers; the clinical judgment of the outside observer of dissociation psychosis, depersonalization, hallucination, and delusion in regard to the subject; the apparent increased muscular strength, and the dissolution and rebuilding of programs and metaprograms by self and by the outside therapist, and so forth.

The increase in white noise energy allows quick and random access to memory and lowers the threshold to unconscious memories—all of which constitutes an expansion of consciousness. In such noise we can project almost anything at almost any cognitive level in almost any allowable mode. One dramatic example is the conviction of some subjects of hearing-seeing-feeling God, when "way out." We project our expectations of God onto the white noise as if the noise were signals so that we hear the voice of God in the Noise. With a bit of proper programming under the right conditions, with the right dose, at the right time, we can program almost anything into the noise within our cognitive limits. The limits are only our own conceptual limits, including limits set by our repressed, inhibited, and forbidden areas of thought. The latter can be analyzed and freed up using the energy of the white noise in the service of the ego, such as a metaprogram to analyze yourself can be part of the instructions to be carried out in the LSD-25 state.

> With a bit of proper programming under the right conditions, with the right dose, at the right time, we can program almost anything into the noise within our cognitive limits.

The noise introduced brings a certain amount of disorder with it, even as white noise in the physical world brings randomness. However, the LSD-25 noise randomizes signals only in a limited way—not enough to destroy all order, only enough to superimpose a small creative "jiggling" on program materials and metaprograms and their signals. This noisy component added to the usual signals in the circuits adds enough uncertainty to the meanings to make new interpretations more probable. If the noise becomes too intense, we might expect it to wipe out information and lead to unconsciousness, and even death, at very high levels.

Signals from Noise

THE MAJOR OPERATIVE PRINCIPLE SEEMS TO BE that the human biocomputer operates in such a way as to make signals out of noise and thus to create information out of random energies where there was no signal. This is the *Projection Principle*. Noise is creatively used in non-noise models. The information "created" from the noise can be shown by careful analysis to have been in the storage system of the biocomputer. That is, the projection moves information out of storage into the perception apparatus so that it appears to originate in the chosen "outside" noisily excited system.

Demonstrations of this principle are multifarious. In a single mode, listening to a real acoustic physical white noise in profound isolation in solitude, the void space, we can hear what we want—or fear—to hear, such as human voices talking about us, or our enemies discussing plans, and so forth. With entheogens we can listen to white noise, including very low frequencies, and see desired—or feared—visions projected on the blank screen of our closed eyes. We can detect the noise level of the mind itself and use it for cognitional projections rather than sense-organ-data projections when in the profound isolation of the void space with the silence, darkness and isothermal skin conditions of water suspension in solitude. Instead of seeing or hearing the projected data, we feel and think it.

This is one basis of the mistake by certain persons of assuming that the projected thoughts come from outside one's own mind, such as oneness with the universe, the thoughts of God in us, extraterrestrial beings sending thoughts into us, and other such explanations. Because of the lack of sensory stimuli, and lack of normal inputs into the computer—lack of energy in the reality program, the space in the computer usually used for the projection of data from the senses and hence the external world is available substitutively for the display of thinking and feeling.

> The human biocomputer operates in such a way as to make signals out of noise

The occurrence of such spontaneous errors is far from an uncommon event. Conservative estimates suggest about 10^{14} elementary operations per second in a single human brain. If we can believe the work of Hyden and of Pauling these operations are performed on about 10^{21} molecules. From stability considerations, we may estimate that per second from 10^9 to 10^{11} molecules will spontaneously change their quantum state as a result of the tunnel effect. This suggests that from 10^3 to $10^{-1}\%$ of all operations in the brain are afflicted with an intrinsic noise figure which has to be taken care of in one way or another.

The beginning of the 20th century saw the fallacy of our progenitors in their trust in a fixed number of m propositions. This number constantly grows with new discoveries which add new variables to our system of knowledge. In this connection it may amuse you that in order just to keep the logical strength of our wisdom from slipping, the ratio of the rate of coalescing, $\dot{m}$, to the rate of discovery, $\dot{k}$, must okay the inequality

$$\frac{\dot{k}}{\dot{m}} \geq k \cdot \ln 2$$

I have the feeling that today, with our tremendous increase in experimental techniques, m is occasionally so large that the above inequality is not fulfilled, and we are left with more riddles than before.

To this frustration to reach perfect truth we, children of the second half of the 20th Century, have added another doubt. This is the suspicion that noise may enter the most effective coalition, flipping an established "false" into a deceptive "true," or, what might be even worse, flipping an irrelevant "true" into an unwarranted "false."

—Von Foerster
Bio-Logic

Projections

IN SOME CASES the use of visually projected images to aid in seeing the nature of our defensive, evasive, and ideali-

zation mechanisms can be realized during the several hours of the special states of consciousness achieved with the help of potent entheogens. It is possible to induce a special state of consciousness—or a special program or metaprogram in the use of perception circuitry—in which remembered or unconsciously stored images of self or of others appear on or in place of the body image with a mirror for the careful inspection of the whole body or the face alone in the external reality. Such stored images can be selected within certain limits, manipulated within other limits, or allowed to occur in a free-association context, appearing as parallels of the current thought-stream.

Orders to self for the appearance of these phenomena may resemble the posthypnotic suggestion instructions given during auto-hypnosis, the metaprogrammatic instruc-tions to a very large biocomputer for a certain type of display program with special content to be displayed, and the orders to a large organization to produce a play with many actors operating in one place in space, one after the other, each with an assigned role not necessarily specified in detail. Such projections can be maintained for periods of about 30 minutes of objective time and worked with in the self-analysis context.

At the end of this time-interval some fatigue is noted with subsequent stopping of the display. Re-evocation can be achieved after a period of rest from this and similar tasks for a period of 15 minutes objective time. Several such periods can be evoked during a single intense entheogenic reprogramming session.

Projected Face

THE CURRENT AFFECT and its modulation by conscious wishing is immediately shown on the facial expression of the projection despite a lack of change in the objective face itself. The projected face and real face fit together in three dimensions. It is almost as if the perception systems were using the real face and recomputing it to give a different appearance. That is, if the real face is held neutral then the projected face will manipulate the apparent features of the real face with accurate showing of anger, joy, sexual desire, hatred, jealousy, pleasure, pain, fear, psychic mutilation of ego, adoration of self, and several other such emotions. These have been studied by their mirror-projections.

Processing Conflicts

CONFLICTS CAN BE PROJECTED IN SEVERAL WAYS. The images switch rapidly back and forth between the two conflicting categories, emotions, orders, persons, ideals, or other. Alternatively, disparate parts of the internalized argument are projected side by side, giving a peculiar stereoscopic depth-in-conflict appearance to the display. Profound fatigue shows by showing aged or diseased splotchy images.

The negative operations which prevent certain contents from reaching access to the display mechanism can be shown to exist by using alternate "acceptable-to-the-ego-ideal" routes to the display program and its projection. For example, material which cannot be projected onto your own mirrored image, sometimes can be projected onto a color picture of someone else. In some cases the other person in the picture is most suitably and acceptably of the opposite sex—face alone, full body clothed, or unclothed—for the full use of the display of the desired material.

In the proper circumstances a properly selected real person can also serve as the external reality three-dimensional screen onto which material can be projected. This latter "screen" is not a passive one and may say or do something on its own which either changes the projection or invokes a new program—such as the demanding external reality program, which may abolish the whole phenomenon of projection in the visual display itself. When we see a visual projection onto the face of another person of our true deeper feelings, the realization may come that this happens to us all the time below the levels of awareness without the special powers attributable to the entheogenic substance. That is, there is an already prepared unconscious "display," which is here allowed access to the visual mechanism by the special conditions, that normally operates in the external reality program with other persons unconsciously or preconsciously. This first-time finding can have therapeutic benefits in the consequent self-analysis of our human relations.

Corporeal Face

ONE INTERESTING KIND OF A PROJECTION onto the image of your own whole body or onto the real body of another is the phenomenon of the self-creation of the corporeal face. In this phenomenon, you see a face of a monstrous being whose projected features are made up of real body parts. The shoulders become the top of head, mammal areola become "oculi" (with female, proptosis), navel to "nares," pubes to "mouth," and with male, penis to "lingua."

This face, though quite vacuous of itself, can be made frightening, sad or happy with proper programming. Once seen, it is easily programmed, even with extreme body position changes. Analysis shows, in a particular case, that this face is in storage from very young childhood and was resulted from fantasies about bodies, male and female, threatening or seductive. This projection is useful in tracing the origins of certain fears.

The Blank Screen

THE EXTERNAL REALITY SCREENS for the projection of the display program in the entheogenic state can be arranged in a set with dimensions relating each to the others. These include non-self-real persons, motion pictures of these persons in various states, and still pictures of the persons. Also included are pictures of self from the past, motion and still pictures, three dimensional and flat, here-and-now three-dimensional color images of your face and/ or body in a mirror. Finally, it includes the eye-open or eyes-closed blank unlighted or lighted projection screen.

The blank projection screen introspectively considered varies upon whether the eyes are open or closed. In the absolute dark, we can detect differences between eyes open and the eyes closed blank screen. In the eyes opens case there is a feeling of depth out beyond the eyes—a feeling of a real visual space. By contrast, the eyes closed immediately turns the vision to a different visual space that seems more internal, more introspective, and more subjective. These differences are attenuated in the entheogenic state.

The blank screen is the most difficult one to work with but is the least "driving" of the group. The blank screen interferes least with our creative efforts. It takes more program circuitry to create those aspects that can be furnished by the other screens themselves, from the perception mechanisms directly into the projection program itself. The blank screen does not so easily show the forbidden transitions except by remaining blank. That is, more relaxation and freedom to free associate with this visual mode is required to project on to a blank screen.

Sources of Input

Cross-model synesthetic projection may help with the blank screen. Excitation coming in hearing mechanisms can excite visual projection. Music is the commonest excitation used. The well-organized patterned input of music tends to "drive the content by association." For instance, religious music can evoke religious visions constructed in childhood from real pictures, churches, fantasies, and religious experiences.

Voices, such as your own real or recorded voice or the voice of another person, are another source of input. These sources can have problems similar to those with the pictures. The high priority program we are calling the *external reality program* may tend to usurp the circuitry and take over from the projection program with pictures or voices of known and valued persons, which interrupts the projection and its free association. The relevance of external reality's content and its connections can be clarified with self-analysis, using techniques of psychoanalysis and other self-exploratory approaches.

Such interruptions depend upon the individual biocomputer and its conflicts in relation to the projection program versus the external reality program. When guilt or fear is present, the external sources attract the energy of the biocomputer back to the external reality. Alternatively, if the level of excitation from the person in the external reality rises above a certain value, the whole biocomputer will be turned to that particular person's vocal output and behaviors.

Purely random noise may avoid these difficulties. It may be a proper acoustically lighted blank screen for cross-model excitation of the visual projections. Initial experiments with inphase and non-phase noise in the two ears show some programming possibilities. One pitfall is to avoid programming by the random processes of the noise itself, which tends to result in chaotic programming. Randomness itself can build up to a large intensity within the metaprogramming systems. With adjustment of the acoustic intensity of the two non-phase related noises these effects can be attenuated and the noisily lighted visual screen used for proper projection purposes. My experiments were only preliminary. I leave this for others to explore.

Zero Level External Reality

WHEN SUFFICIENT PROGRESS HAS BEEN ACHIEVED with the external reality projection screens of the various kinds—visual, acoustic to visual synesthetic, body image, and others—the elimination of sensory stimulation from the external reality allows deeper direct penetration into the unconscious. When in the void state of sensory isolation more circuitry in our huge computer is freed up from the external excitation programs. This enables more circuitry to be devoted to the internal cognitive reality and its analysis. The projection program is still used, but in a somewhat different way.

Interlock
External Reality Program

Systems

1. Afferent
2. Efferent
3. Reticular modulating +/-
4. Positive system phasing
5. Negative system phasing
6. Cortical storage and programming
7. Built-in programs

Ideal Conditions

A MAXIMALLY ATTENUATED ENVIRONMENT is 92 to 95 degrees F. isothermal skin, saltwater suspension, zero light levels, near-zero sound levels, without clothes, without wall or floor contacts, in solitude in remote isolation—the void space. This environment is found in the sensory isolation tank which I described in *The Quiet Center*. When in such a sensory void environment for several hours, the addition of a powerful entheogen allows us to see that all the previous experiences with "outside screens" are evasions of deeper penetration of self and hence are screens in the sense of "blocking the view behind," as well as "receiving the projected images".

15
Logic System

OR THE SAKE OF CLARITY the following presentation of the logic employed in this paper is given. It is quite apparent that there is at least a four-value logic employed by the biocomputer. There are the usual "true" and "false" values. In addition there is another pair that can be called "as if true" and "as if false". Each of these four values can be applied to the external reality and to the internal reality of the human biocomputer.

In the internal reality case there is a metaprogram for each of these values, which can be stated as "define as true—or false—a given metaprogram." A less intense metaprogram is "defined as if true a given metaprogram or defined as if false a given metaprogram." In the experiments on basic beliefs, "if defined as "true" then the metaprogram is "true" within limits to be determined."

These various values may be modified with a judgment of their probability and with the defining of the desired intensity. The probability scale is 1.0 for absolutely

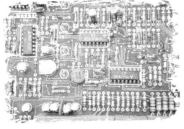 certain, a gradation of probability down to the value 0, which is improbable and to -1 for impossible. Such values are applied to each of the four logic categories with regard to a specific metaprogram.

True Programs

SUCH A LOGIC SYSTEM CAN BE SEEN OPERATING in the external human reality in coalitions of various sorts. A coalition can function "as if an internal judgment" in the sense that it defines certain things as "true" which are then true within limits to be determined. The usual structure of human law seems to share this property. The concept of consensus wisdom includes this logic system.

There are certain metaprograms and programs which have an imperative, externally-proven truth-falsity relationship which cannot be manipulated within the human biocomputer without danger to its existence. These metaprograms and programs can be considered as imperatives from some parts of the program level of the human biocomputer which must function as supra-self-metaprograms, that is, there must be recognition of the built-in or hardwired necessary-for-survival nature of these pro-grams.

Some of these true programs are yet to be determined in biological science. The following have been determined. The necessity of obtaining food in response to hunger, the necessity of sexual activities and pleasure, adequate responses to pain and fear, such as freeze, flee, or fight.

Programs designed for survival of the body in a gravitational field take up a large fraction of the apparatus and of the time and energy of the human computer. The physiological limits of stimulation of the special senses must be closely maintained—not too high or too low levels of light, sound, and so forth. External temperatures and internal temperatures must be regulated within certain limits. Illnesses introduce new programs, including those illnesses which are the result of self- multiprogramming.

Direct physical injury with physical trauma to the body have their own imperatives. The intake of certain gases into the respiratory system must be regulated very cautiously. Among these are oxygen, carbon dioxide, water vapor, carbon monoxide, nitrogen, xenon, krypton, nitrous oxide, and so forth. There are programs regulating the amount of liquid surrounding the body, such as to avoid drowning, the amount of solids piled on top of the body to avoid crushing, the total pressures of gases around the body, neither too much nor too little, the level of radiation, the level of elementary particles from outer space, or from artificial sources. The various kinds of viruses, bacteria, fungi, algae, protozoa, and so forth, must be carefully regulated by proper programming.

> There are such phenomena as "information-overload" and "information-deprivation."

Interactions of the human computer with other mammals and with supra-mammalian species must be programmed in an anticipatory way. There must be regulation of information, the kind of information and the amounts from anywhere and from anyone for the best functioning of the human computer. There are such phenomena as "information-overload" and "information-deprivation." There are multiple programs for the regulation of the individual with respect to the society surrounding him, which have their own imperatives.

In summary, there are metaprograms that must be assumed to be true in the sense of external reality and external proof. Each of these metaprograms has its own definition of that which is true or false. The "as if true" and "as if false" categories can only be applied to these metaprograms in temporary hypothetical consideration of their content but not in their performance in the real biocomputer and in the real world. During the entheogenic state certain of these programs must be considered as true—externally true and provable—in order to survive during the entheogenic experience.

Hardware-Software Relationships

SEVERAL ASSUMPTIONS ARE NEEDED to investigate the complex relationships between the metaprograms, programs and the neuronal activity in the central nervous system.

Assumptions

Assume an array of approximately 10^{10} neurons connected in the particular ways they are in the central nervous system.

Assume that the particular critical events in each neuron is the firing of an impulse into its axon.

Assume a method of control of this firing from outside the CNS.

Assume a method of pickup of the impulse discharged which can be transmitted to the outside of the CNS.

Assume that each impulse of each neuron in the 10^{10} array is recorded in a high-speed computer outside the CNS.

Assume that storage of the time of occurrence of each impulse is stored as a separate datum.

Assume that for every second there are 10^{14} such impulses stored from the total CNS.

Assume that this external computer can, in a subsequent time period over 10^{10} channels, reproduce the time pattern of impulses stored, in the same time pattern in which they came into storage.

Test by a Behavioral Technique.

THE PRESENT THEORY STATES that behavior of the organism during the time of reproduction of the pattern will be very closely identical with the original occurrence of the behavior. This hypothesis can be tested as follows. During a time in which the organism containing the biocomputer is doing some complex behavior such as speaking a sentence and writing a sentence at the same time, record completely the external behavior on video, multiple channel tape or other device. Store all of the neural signs of activity during the time of production of speech and of the writing. In a subsequent time period, play back or call up from storage the patterns that were stored in the same sequence and put them out from the computer over 10^{10} channels into the CNS.

Record the subsequent behavior and compare this record with the previous external record of the behavior when the sentence was being produced. If the original hypothesis is correct, the two patterns of behavior as captured by cameras and sound recorders will be identical. If something else is operating in the computer other than control by neural impulses, the two behaviors will have differences, depending on the extent of the control. It may be that longer time patterns are needed to control all of the feedbacks—with, say, the endocrine and bio-chemical systems that have longer time constants than the proposed experiment. There may need to be preconditioning periods, which are also stored, before the two behavior sequences can be made identical.

Basic Questions

WITH THIS MODEL, we can ask many basic questions. For example, what is the physical set of events which gives rise to phenomena in the area of the phoneme, in the area of semantic levels of abstraction, in the areas of metaprogramming outside, and the use of language for programming?

With this technique, evaluation of drug effects on the central nervous system can yield meaningful insight into the critical physical events taking place in the CNS. Analyses can be made of the kinds of programming and metaprogramming that take place in separate systems of the brain, such as the neocortex, the meso-, paleo-, and archeo-cortices versus the subcortical systems such as the thalmus, the hypothalamus, and the mesencephalon, for example. A systems analysis is then possible of the limbic system, the positively reinforcing and negatively reinforcing systems, the control of the pituitary, and the feedback control by the contents of the blood of the various parts of the CNS. Evaluation of the feedback relationships between all of these systems can then be specified in a quantitative way.

This formulation objectifies the subjective in a way in which experiments can be designed, not only to store the objective aspects of subjective events, but also to reproduce the subjective events from storage. It permits quantitative analysis of the physical aspects of the subjective events outside of the CNS that originally created them.

This formulation permits experiments in which a given CNS can control most of the functions of a second CNS. The corresponding parts of the second CNS as compared to the first can be found and an evaluation made of the differences in thresholds, in area distributions of thresh-olds and in analo-gous areas between the two CNS's. These are exciting possibilities that will tell us much.

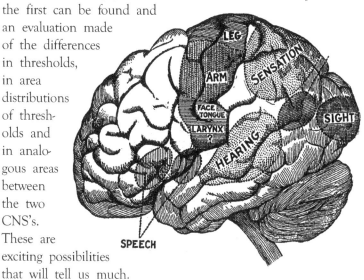

SPEECH

Metaprogramming the Positive States

LSD-25 AND SIMILAR POWERFUL ENTHEOGENS FACILITATE the positive reinforcement systems in the CNS and inhibit the punishment systems in the CNS. Powerful entheogens add noise at all levels, decreasing many thresholds in the CNS. The apparent strengths of programs below the usual levels of awareness increase. Programmability of metaprograms—suggestibility—increases, allowing more programming by the self-metaprogram and external sources.

The continuous positive state—positive reinforcement, reward, pleasure—plus inhibited negative system activity causes increased positive reinforcement of self, of our thinking, of thinking introduced by other persons in external reality and any given patterned complex input, such as music, paintings, photos, and so forth. Subsequent to exposure, the effects fall off slowly over a two- to six-weeks period. Residual effects can be detected up to one year.

Repeated exposures at weekly to biweekly periods for several months or years maintain the above reinforcements when the above conditions, inputs and outputs can be reproduced. There is reinforcement of the positive reinforcements until the usual state before entheogens becomes negative.

16
Evasions

 EVASION, AS I AM USING IT HERE, is meant to imply a similar concept to defensive maneuvers identified in psychoanalytic literature. Evasions include any program or metaprogram entered upon to avoid, to hide, or to distort a deeper program or metaprogram that is too seductive, threatening or chaotic for the self-programmer to deal with.

At the beginning of a profound isolation or void session many people experience a fear that is disembodied, with no referents in the external reality. With experience this fear is revealed to be a fear of our own inner unknowns. After a thorough exploration of our various evasive metaprograms, we realize that the only thing to fear in the void is fear itself—in overwhelming amounts. With sufficient training we can convert the emotion from a negative to positive motivational dynamic.

> The only thing to fear in the void is fear itself—in overwhelming amounts.

The question as to whether or not we must go through negative emoting in order to experience enough of the punishing aspects to avoid them is moot. It takes self-discipline to pursue the negatively tinged programs and metaprograms stored in memory. Hedonistic withdrawal from further consideration of unpleasant events and memories is tempting but these escapes into pleasure are evasions of further self-analysis. As we clear up unpleasant programs and metaprograms, our control of pleasurable programming and metaprogramming can itself become a seductive evasion of self-analysis.

Unconsciously operating taboos, denials and inhibitions are revealed by the absence of consciously desired and ordered projections in certain areas. Areas of unconscious elaboration show as projections of great detail and completeness even though no real remembered reality could possibly correspond to the projection. Screen memories show in great profusion. As the buried material behind the screen is uncovered, the screen memory disappears.

Flickering Images Phenomena

AN APPARENT DEFENSIVE MANEUVER is the flickering images phenomena. New images come at such a rapid rate—2 or 3 per second—like a slowed flickering movie in which you cannot inspect any one image long enough to recognize its significance. Another evasion is the melting, or mosaic, or distortion maneuver in which images flow in whole or plastically, or are broken up into parts like a mosaic, or parts are interchanged among several stored images at different levels. The melting, mosaic or distortion can itself be programmed under direct orders. It is only considered an evasion when it is not under the control of the self.

The use of any external reality screen in the profound isolation of zero level external reality situation is a defensive maneuver to avoid visualizing or experiencing what we fear most in the deeper levels of our computer—in the unconscious. Using screens is necessary and useful on the way in and to return for confirmation of the findings at later times.

Seduction of Pleasure

TOO FREQUENT USE OF ENTHEOGENS MUST BE AVOIDED. Long periods of interlock with the external reality is needed. It may take months to integrate your findings with the real world as you have chosen to live in it.

The easily evoked pleasure of the entheogenic state may be a major goal for some persons. The external reality struggle to obtain pleasure from the environment has rules of its own which must be met realistically and with intelligence and balance. Discipline in the self-metaprogrammer is absolutely essential when exploring the further reaches of consciousness and alternative realities. Further progress in self-analysis cannot be made without self-discipline. To prevent getting seduced by an entheogenically induced state of pleasure, it is wise to avoid further experiments for several weeks, even several months, while reasserting the natural accesses to pleasure in external reality.

> Too frequent use of entheogens must be avoided. Long periods of interlock with the external reality is needed.

An apparently paradoxical situation exists in the profound void situation. We can pursue self-analysis and access to the keys to pleasure within our self and keys to lessening the pain and fear in our self. However, once we have unlocked the pleasure and attenuated the pain we must use the resulting released energies and attach them somehow to the external reality programs and the ideals—supra-self-metaprograms—which we have set up. We do not dissipate all of this pleasure in hedonistic and narcissistic gratification.

A pitfall of entheogenic experiences, especially with LSD-25, which I used predominantly in my void space research, is exactly this—we can stay in an expanded state of pleasure for several hours. This can become quite seductive so that the explorer becomes lazy and returns to this state at every opportunity. Doing so is the experience of ecstasy, or bliss, or the transcendent state sought by the religious proponents of the using entheogens for religious purposes—but it is not the rigorous self-analysis necessary for conscious self-programming.

These findings are very similar if not identical to those found in classical psychoanalysis. After repressions and denials are released during the analysis, the access of pleasurable activity increases rapidly. The same temptations exist to become a pleasure-seeking organism. This is a seduction—a trap—for the explorer who must analyze this tendency to get beyond it and back onto the path of discovery.

When comparing the classical analytical situation to solitudinous self-analysis in the void space we must be quite aware of what has been sacrificed in each case. The advantage of an external analyst listening to you producing the material is that what you avoid can be pointed out rapidly before you became too involved in the evasions. On the other hand, the analyst's interpretations can distract you from pursuing in depth certain aspects of your own self-analysis. Even solitudinous self-analysis while using entheogens should be referred back to an external analyst at times, especially after large amounts of powerfully acting unconscious programs have been unearthed. As happens during classical analysis, some programs may be acted out after profound solitude experiences. This is one of the risks and the gambles of this technique.

Inside Analyst

EXPLORERS ARE ENCOURAGED to become sophisticated in psychoanalysis itself. During classical psychoanalysis we begin to modify our biocomputer and the self-programmer to include the methods of computation that our analysts use. Through modeling we incorporate a metaprogram of self-analysis which models our analysts' methods. In classical psychoanalytic terms, we tend to incorporate aspects of our analysts. When a satisfactorily functioning internal analyst—an analytical metaprogram—for the self-metaprogram has evolved, we can launch on our own, no longer needing the external analyst to the same degree that we did earlier. Our analysis proceeds from the analyst outside to the analyst inside.

When using entheogens in the profound isolation of the void space our biocomputer uses certain parts of itself for transformations and projections of data from memory into systems stimulated by energies coming from the external world. Such projections are easier to achieve than when these systems are not excited by energies coming from the outside world. The major reason for inability to project on the blank screens is fear of what lies underneath, below the levels of awareness. As these fears are analyzed and shown to be peculiarly childlike and childish, we can proceed in our exploration.

Inner Cognition Space

As WE PROCEED from outer or external projection analysis to internal projection analysis, we move from external excitation of projection systems to a lack of excitation. For example, in the profound blackness and darkness of the floatation tank—my void space—there is no visual stimulus coming to the visual system—my eyes. Similarly in the profound silence there are no sounds coming into the acoustic apparatus—my ears. The other sensory systems are at a very low level of stimulation from the external world.

You might expect then that these systems would appear to be absolutely quiet, dark and empty. This is not so. In the absence of external excitations coming through the natural end organs the perception systems maintain activity. Excitation comes from other parts of the computer—from program storage and from internal body sources of excitation. At first, the self-programmer interprets these perceptual spaces as if it were coming from outside. In other words, the self interprets the sources of the excitation as if coming from the "real" world. For certain persons and personalities this is a very disturbing experience.

Trouble for Explorers

THIS IS WHERE MANY BEGINNING EXPLORERS get into trouble and where psychiatric and clinical judgments may interfere with the natural development of the phenomena. From babyhood we have learned that this kind of phenomena, in a totally conscious individual, is somehow forbidden, antisocial and possibly even psychotic. To move beyond this obstacle we must analyze the metaprogram that has been implanted in us from childhood and examine its rationality or lack of same. The explorer must proceed in spite of this kind of psychiatric interpretation of the phenomena.

We must neutralize clinical psychiatric explanations and judgments about these phenomena. If we assume that going through these phenomena is a dangerous procedure in which we might become enamored of them and hence get into an irreversible psychosis, we can be kept from experiencing these phenomena directly. The necessary and sufficient conditions for the induction of a psychosis are not yet understood, so we should not jump to the conclusion that these phenomena themselves are or can cause a psychosis. It may be that professional fear is preventing our further analysis of these phenomena. *This work is not done on the fly.* The issue of insight into our own mental processes, the issue of self-discipline and inspecting and understanding these processes are at stake here. Professionals and others who believe that there is a psychosis impending in normal people have definite troubles with these kinds of phenomena. Heuristically such beliefs weaken our self-discipline under these circumstances and make us rather unfit for serious exploration.

When we realize that this is an evasion or a defensive maneuver against seeing the true state of affairs we can allow our self to go on and to experience the deeper set of phenomena without interfering with the natural metaprograms. After achieving this level of freedom from anxiety we can then go on to the next stages. This work is not done on the fly. Programming orders for these inner happenings to take place are worked out in advance of the exploration session and written down or spoken into a recorder. As the explorer becomes more skilled such orders can be programmed without external aids.

Here is one explorer's phenomenological description of the experience:

I experienced an immediate internal reality that was postulated by the self. It is apparent to me that my assumptions about this experience generated the whole experience. The experience affected the apparent appearance of other persons, the appearance of other beings not human, my own past fantasies, and my own self-analysis. Each can be programmed to happen in interaction with those parts of my self beyond my conscious awareness.

Content experienced under these conditions lacks strong reality clues. Externally real displays are not furnished. The excitation from the reality outside does not pattern the displays. Therefore the projections which do occur are from those systems at the next inward level from the operations of the perception apparatus devoted to external reality.

Here's how another explorer described the phenomena that ensued.

The visualization is immersed in darkness in three dimensions at times but only when I evade the emerging multidimensional cognitive and cognitive space. I am aware of "the silence" in the hearing sphere. This too gives way to the new space which is developing. My body image fluctuates, appearing and disappearing, as fear or other need builds up. As with the darkness and the silence so with the presence or absence of my body image.

Progress in using these projection spaces is measured by our ability to neither project external reality data from storage into these spaces nor to project into these spaces the absence of external reality stimuli. We can project living images or external reality equivalents, or we can project blackness or the absence of external reality images. We can project definite sounds, such as voices or an as if external reality, or we can project silence—the absence of sound—in the external reality. We can project body image such as seeing oneself flexing one's muscles to reassure ourselves that the image is functioning with real feedback or we can have a perception of a lack of the body image.

In each of these dichotomized situations we are really projecting external reality and its equivalents—positive or negative. To experience the next set of phenomena we must work through these dichotomous symbols of the external world and realize that they are evasions of further penetration to deeper levels.

In summary then we start on the deeper journeys, independently, metaprogrammed properly, and relatively safe but without evasions. After having been through some of the innermost depths of self, a result is that they are only our own beliefs and their multitudes of randomized logical consequences deep down inside self. There is nothing else but stored experience.

Extinguishing Programs

AS THE EXPLORER BECOMES SKILLED in these realms, it becomes possible to use the principles of Pavlovian and Skinnerian programming to extinguish or erase unwanted programs. For example, becoming anxious may have been programmed to the color green. This program can be erased by calling up screen memories of green while remaining completely relaxed. After doing this many times, the pairing of green and anxiety is replaced by green being paired with relaxation and the old, dysfunctional program is erased. This is a process called "desensitization," which is based on Pavlovian programming principles.

On the other hand, an anxious response program may be being maintained by reinforcing consequences. For example, when Little Albert sees Santa's whiskers he becomes anxious and cries. Albert's crying is followed by his mother soothing him and giving him a lollipop—two powerfully reinforcing consequences. A program maintained by positive reinforcement can be extinguished by replacing the reinforcement with no response. The self-programmer can manipulate consequences by using screen memories and then projecting a new result—no response from the mother and no lollipop. If, in external reality, Little Albert's crying-for-attention-and-a-lollipop program has been maintained by random, intermittent reinforcement, it will take many reruns of the scenario without his mother's comfort and a lollipop before the program is erased because it has become resistent to extinction.

A hidden danger in this approach is that withholding an anticipated positive reinforcement is experienced as punishment by the biocomputer. Using punishment to erase programs is unpredictable and can lead to the establishment of evasions programs.

Another approach is to call up the anxiety-provoking screen memory and then to experience the anxiety until it dissipates—to face the fear. This is not so easy to do. Escaping-avoiding anxiety is a built-in program. You must override this hardwired program and hold yourself in the high anxiety-state in order to erase anxiety programs. The reason is that anything that removes or turns off a negative is reinforcing. This principle of *negative reinforcement* is the process operating in the joke in which a man who is banging his head is asked why and answers, "because it feels so good when I stop."

In short, each time we evade anxiety in external reality or in screen memories, we reinforce the anxiety program because it feel so good when we turn off or avoid anxiety. Such a program is very resistant to extinction.   One way to erase the program is to call up an anxiety-provoking image onto your Blank Screen and to hold yourself in the anxious state until the anxiety dissipates, and to repeat this procedure until the screen memory is no longer able to trigger anxiety.   This process is sometimes called "implosion."

Another technique is to alter your behavior in the screen memory and then simulate rewarding consequences for this more desirable behavior. For example, Little Albert could call up a screen memory of the soothing experience of his mother's attention and then create simulations of alternative behaviors, such as smiling and saying, "I'm a big boy" and then create a simulation of his mother providing soothing attention.   These are but a few of the infinite ways that an explorer can use programming principles to erase unwanted old programs and to self-program one's biocomputer in desired ways.

Boundless Self

WHEN WE ABANDON THE USE OF PROJECTION of external reality equivalents, new phenomena appear. Thought and feeling take over the spaces formerly occupied by external reality equivalents. There is a sense of infinity. We have the feeling that self extends infinitely out in all directions. The self is still centered at one place but its boundaries have disappeared and it moves out in all directions and extends to fill the limits of the universe as far as we know them. The explanation of this phenomenon is that we have taken over the perception spaces and filled them with programs, metaprograms, and self-metaprograms, which are modified in the inner perception to be "as if external reality equivalents." To be appreciated, this transformation—this special mental state—must be experienced directly. Nighttime dreams have something of this quality and show this kind of a phenomenon.

Various evasions of realization of what is happening can take place. We can imagine we are traveling through the real universe, flying past suns and galaxies. We can imagine we are communicating with other beings in these other universes. We may experience an oceanic feeling, a oneness with the universe, and a fusing with Universal Mind. Scientifically speaking, it is fairly obvious that we are not doing any of these things and that our basic beliefs determine what we experience.

A more objective description would be that the ordinary perception and projection spaces are filled with cognition and conation processes. These states—or "direct perceptions of reality" as some call them—are our thoughts and feelings expanding into the circuitry that is usually occupied by perception of external reality. In our biocomputer this holds for each and every mode, including vision, audition, proprioception, and so forth.

Unless we can move philosophically and scientifically far enough to see the utility of going through these experiences there can be a rapid withdrawal, a faulting out of self from the whole project. We are not willing to undergo the fantasy dangers that we set up ahead of time. Worries tend to revolve around maintaining insight into these processes once under the influence of the entheogen.

Brain and Mind Injury

CANDIDLY CONSIDERED we may ask if the entheogenic substance under these conditions changes our brain and mind structure irreversibly out of our control? The proper controlled research on whether or not there are permanent changes in brains has not been done on animals' nor on humans' brains. So there definitely is a risk in this area. Is one willing to gamble on this particular risk? It is wise for the explorer to face up to these questions candidly, honestly, and ruthlessly. The explorer is moving into an area which is filled with unknowns of primary importance.

The issue of brain and mind injury as a result of using entheogens such as LSD-25 and MDMA also called "ecstasy," has not been thoroughly researched and has not been faced by recreational enthusiasts. It is an issue constantly raised by those in opposition to their use. The science of finding out whether or not there is any truth in either side, pro or con, has been lacking. The pro-group tries to do spectacular things. The con-group looks askance at the enthusiasm of the other group and claims that they have lost their insight and are hedonistically overvaluing the effects experienced subjectively. The contra-group claims brain damage and/or mind damage. The pro-group claims basic understanding of the mind, a new understanding of mental diseases, and a new approaches to the psychotherapy of recalcitrant diseases, such as alcoholism, as well as artistic, religious, and philosophical claims. The turning point between the pros and cons of the use of entheogens hinges philosophically at the edge of this cognitive-conative projection space phenomena. Do we lose our insight and initiative by going here? This question should be asked and answered scientifically and experimentally.

17
Coalitions
& Interlock

HE PHENOMENON OF COMPUTER INTERLOCK facilities model instruction and operation. One computer interlocks with one or more other computers above and below the level of awareness any time the communicational distance is sufficiently small to bring the interlock functions above threshold level.

In the complete physical absence of other external computers within the critical interlock distance, the self-directed and other-directed programs can be clearly detected, analyzed, recomputed, and reprogrammed, and new metaprograms initiated by the solitudinous computer itself in the void space. In this physical reality, which is an environment as completely attenuated with solitude as possible, maximum intensity, maximum complexity, and maximum speed of reprogramming are achievable by the self.

In the field of scientific research, such a computer can function in many different ways—from the pure, austere thought processes of theory and mathematics to the almost random data absorption of the naturalistic approach with newly-found systems, or to the coordinated interlock with other human computers of an engineering effort.

Von Foerster defines coalitions as large aggregates of connected matter. Living systems are coalitions par excellence. A protozoan is a coalition of atoms and molecules forming membranes and sub-micro and micro structures which reproduce by collecting the same kinds of atoms and molecules from the environment to form new identical individuals. A sponge is a primitive coalition of protozoa with enhanced survival over any one protozoan. A man is a tightly organized coalition of cells, including some mobile protozoa—lymphocytes, macrophages, oligoden-droglia, and so on. Von Foerster says that mammalian cells of Homo sapiens may be the most numerous cells on earth. These cells with their multiple level coalitions have the longest current survival time.

Organism Models

1. Physical-chemical to quantum mechanical: Series of millisecond to biochemical reserves, physical-chemical flows, energy-force-material exchange with outside sources-sinks; repeatability, reliability, signal/noise relations.

2. Physiological: (Structure and function) Partial integrated-over-time pictures of physical patterns. Net results over seconds to days to years. Organism vs. environment generation of actions, signals.

3. Modern psychological: (Behavior) Selection of certain aspects of physical physiological data and models which show properties of modifiability, CNS model making, model comparison, storage, learning, memory, physchophysical.

4. Classical psychological: (Psyche) Mental, subjective, inside view, psychoanalytic, solipsistic, ego-centered, personal models.

5. Evolutionary: (Origins of life and species) Gradual formation of basic physical-chemical units into organic particles, cells, organisms, formation of genetic codes and cytoplasmic orders; increasing sizes of cellular aggregations; formation of species; changes to new species, evolution of CNS; evolution of man from anthropoids; origins of speech.

6. Social, anthropological: (Pre-historical, historical, current)

8. <u>Religious, mystical</u> (supra-human entities)

7. <u>Basic Particles</u> (Non-human Intelligences)

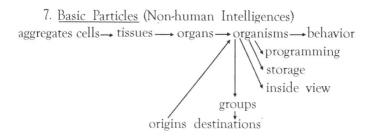

The nature of matter-matter coalitions and cell-cell coalitions and organism-organism coalitions were explored by Von Foerster. For a coalition to exist between any two entities, the dyad is connected by a bond or bonds which reduce the neg-entropy to below the sum of the neg-entropy of each of the two entities separated without a linkage. In this view, the two entities when in coalition reduce the physical information available externally below the levels of that available from the two entities each unlinked and separated. The coalition as it exists thus appears to be something more than the mere sum of isolated parts.

The nature of the linkages in coalitions depends upon the level of aggregations. In a human the coalitions include those between special atoms in spatial arrangements with others, such as alpha helices; special cells in spatial patterns, such as liver and brain; and organism coalition tissues such as circulatory, lymph, and autonomic nervous systems. The bones assure a maintenance of total form of the net coalition of a person under a one g gravitational field. The continuance of important aspects of the individual for inter-organism coalitions is based on shape maintenance despite g forces, radiation, heat, and so on.

More Than the Sum

THE RULES WITHIN COALITIONS are different at each level because each level is somehow more than the sum of its separated individuals. For coalitions to develop between individual humans, linkages of various sorts are developed. Agreements are reached and thus the sources of new information from each member are reduced. To maintain a dyadic coalition, interlock between the two human computers is developed. Each human-to-human interlock is unique. Each interlock is also a function of other current and past interlocks of each member and of learned traditional models.

Coalitions between humans are immense in number and have great complexity in their operations. Each adult individual has linkages extending to literally thousands of other individuals.

Each human-to-human interlock is unique.

The amount of time spent on maintenance of linkages is fantastic. The demands on our selves by the various coalitions uses up most of our awake hours—and possibly most of our sleeping hours, as well.

To clarify the discussion we must carefully distinguish between an interhuman coalition operating here-and-now versus one whose past occurrences in the external reality are modeled in the human biocomputer. The here-and-now operations of the model of a past dyadic coalition can operate in the absence of a current instance of interhuman dyadic coalition—or in its presence.

Model Operates Differently

WITH VIGOROUS CURRENT EXTERNAL REALITY INTERLOCK, the human biocomputer is busy with information exchange at all levels—verbal and nonverbal, digital and analogic, and so on. The model projects expectations and predictions continuously as an interlock develops. The real inputs are compared with computed outputs in all modes.

At the other extreme, an isolated individual in the solitude of the void state does not have a present coalition to work on, in, or with. Past coalitions are projected an new models made by making new coalitions of the old ones. As such new relationships

To maintain a dyadic coalition, interlock between the two human computers is developed.

are established in the biocomputer the person settles logical discrepancies between old models and new ones, tends to abolish discontinuities of the logical consequences, basic belief structures, and the basic beliefs are changed, if necessary, to have fewer discrepancies between the internal models.

Coalitions at all levels—from basic particles, atomic-molecular, to cellular-organismic, to human-human levels—have a polar, opposite, balancing set of forces, energies, drives, motivations. On the basic particle-atomic-molecular coalition level, this set can be called *electric charges*. These electric charges operate by well-known coalitional rules, such as opposite attracts, like repels, quantal energy jumps, and the tunneling effect. On the biological level of cells, the cell-cell coalitions have multifarious possibilities, such as meiosis, mitosis, fission, fusion, positive and negative tropisms, ingestion, excretion, and so on. As long as a cell has its own structure, it maintains only structural relations between molecules in itself. It is said that each and every atom in a cell is eventually exchanged for another new atom. The coalitions of a cell's atoms are temporary and in the mass last a most probable time characteristic of cell and atom types, such as lead in bone versus sodium in brain, for example.

At this cellular level electric charges tend to establish gradients. The gradients vary with internal reality and external reality states. The atoms move in and move out, more or less rapidly depending on cell parts—nucleus, mitochondria, ribosomes, and so forth—and functional locus, such as intracellular fluids versus genic structures.

An intra-organismic cell in mammals, for example, has coalitions with other cells and with the organism. It has orders about its relations with neighbors, its origins, its meiotic or mitotic future if any, its motility or sessility, its electrical activity, its chemical activity, where it stays or where it travels and generally where and when it dies.

Each cell is brought under the mass orders of all of the organism by carefully regulated rules of feedback and interconnections through chemo-physical and cellular means. The high-speed intercellular activity system penetrates most of the organism. The intercellular fluid flow penetrates everywhere and bridges the gap between the cell and the blood carriers. The blood system links the basic chemistry everywhere with transport, such as oxygen from outside, molecules from gut, hormones from pituitary, and so on. At the cellular level in the organism the coalitions are essential, the linkages myriad, and the cell is the well-fed and well-cared for slave of the state—the organism—and is killed if it breaks the orders for its type. Feedback is absolutely limiting here.

At the organism-organism level, somewhat like the cellular level, the coalitions depend on food, on temperature, on gravity, radiation, reproduction, its structure, individuals of other species of life, individuals of its species, communication intra- and inter-species, use of its biocomputer. Human coalitions include building and use of human artifacts from tools to skyscrapers to rockets to nonliving computers, and the control and the creation of human relationships, including money, credit, politics, science, books, periodicals, television, and so on.

A single human organism can have several coalitions to deal with. The first coalition is usually parental, which continues until the parents' death and then continues as internal models. Another type of coalition is male-female relationships, especially the marriage coalition. Male-female coalitions form continuously, at all ages. There are financial coalitions, which include individual income and outgo. The amount of money whose flow is controlled by a given individual is generally a quantitative measure of coalition responsibility delegated to that individual by coalitions of many other individuals. An individual can be the controller of a financial coalition only with multiple consents and, hence, control the flow of money into and out of that coalition.

Children represent an important coalition group. Exciting demanding coalitions develop with our offspring. It is a challenge to renew and improve your coalition with each child as the child grows and expands his or her coalition powers.

Unconscious Coalitions

UNCONSCIOUS COALITIONS below the levels of awareness also exist. We expect certain kinds of conditions in our coalitions. Some wishful thinking is expended in fantasized linkages. Contracts as written usually do not—cannot—incorporate explicit statements of unconscious commitments and desires. However, a contract can be misused in the service of wishful thinking—the courts see numerous cases of this kind.

The problems attendant upon breaking human-human coalitions can be smoothly worked out, or be somewhat energetic, or can generate much heat, smoke and fire. The real bond energy left in the linkages usually can be dissipated at any rate desired. The fuss and furor seems to be directly proportional to the energy in the bond and to the rate of bond dissolution—directly proportioned to the time taken and energy spent to obtain agreement on both sides of the human-human linkage. But the rate of control and the necessities of agreement to break the coalition must be dispassionately and objectively evaluated. Unless coalition partners know how to control the results, their desire is to avoid exciting protohuman survival programs below the levels of awareness in the parties in the coalition. These programs require continuous care and maintenance.

Some essential factors of all human-human coalitions are circular feedback, distance rules, positive-attractive and negative-repulsive motives, excitation and inhibition rules and limits, and coalition field agreements. Each human coalition is formed in a coalition field surrounded by other coalitions with other individuals and with institutional agents. The connectivity of a given coalition with all other coalitions is multiple and complex. We are born and raised in a coalition field, which is dynamic and growing. In this field the coalitions vary over a great range of apparent durations. Some coalitions are made to last beyond a single human lifetime; others to last a few minutes or hours or days or weeks.

Freed Bond Energy

THE FREED BOND ENERGY FROM A BROKEN COALITION is used to form new coalitions, or to strengthen others. A resignation, for example, is preferable to a firing. A new pair of necessary coalitions can take the place of the old one with overlap and without break in services. Or the duties of the old coalition are distributed over others.

The bond energies in human coalitions are of two types—attractive and repulsive. To maintain a viable coalition these links must be excited and inhibited by each member within certain limits of time, intensity, rate, and so forth. Sometimes a coalition has aspects of two persons pulling one another together with two ropes and simultaneously pushing one another apart with two poles. The coalition requires adjustment and readjustment of the two pushes and the two pulls involved in the double-bind.

Individual Responsibility

OUR CONCEPT OF INDIVIDUAL HUMAN RESPONSIBILITY rests on the above mappings of multilevel coalitions at each developmental age of the human being. Responsibility starts with a satisfactory coalition between your self and the demanding 10^{12} cells of your body. Responsibility continues with human-human coalitions, with interspecies coalitions from immunity to bacteria, to eating plants and animals, to interspecies communication; with concepts of self including origins, maintenance, progress, destinations; and strong open communication of your self with your innermost realities.

Multiple levels of responsibility and a strong autonomous character are needed to pursue this research. In order to function effectively in human society the depths of the mind must be functioning relatively smoothly under the guidance of the self. To develop this degree of smooth function may require strong measures. These measures require strong educated handling.

18
InterSpecies Interlock

STRUGGLED WITH THE PROBLEMS of devising working models of the interspecies communication problem at a relatively high structured cognitive level. There is no available adequate theory of the human portion of the interspecies communication network such as Man-Dolphin. The major portion of the total problem has been found to be the human species, rather than the dolphinic ones. The lack of such a theory has made it difficult for most scientists to see the reality of the problems posed in the interspecies program.

Little credence can be obtained for the proposition that a problem of interspecies communication exists so long as the conscious-unconscious basic belief of the preeminence of the human brain and mind over all other earthside brains and minds exist. Despite arguments based on the complexity and size of certain nonhuman mammalian brains little if any general belief in the project has been instilled in the scientific community at large. There has been support for further examination and demonstra-

tion of the large dolphin brain with its detailed excellence of structure. There is no lack of interest in this area. The faulting out comes in obtaining competent working scientists' operating interest in evaluating the performance of these large brains. Interest and commitment of time and self are needed for progress.

I aimed to devise a program of encouragement for creating some models of the human end of the interspecies system to illustrate, elucidate, and elaborate the basic assumptions needed to encourage interest and needed research.

Each mammalian brain functions as a computer with properties, programs and metaprograms, partly to be defined and partly to be determined by observation. The human computer contains at least 13 billions of active elements, and hence is functionally and structurally larger than any artificially built computer. This human computer has the properties of modern artificial computers of large size plus additional ones not yet achieved in the non-biological machines. The human computer has stored program properties. Stored metaprograms are also present. Among the suggested properties are self-programming and self-metaprogramming

Programming and metaprogramming language is different for each human depending upon developmental, experiential, genetic, educational, accidental, and self-chosen variables and elements and values. Basically the verbal forms for programming are those of the native language of the individual modulated by nonverbal language elements acquired in the same epochs of the development of that individual.

Computer Interlock

THE PHENOMENON OF COMPUTER INTERLOCK facilitates mutual model construction and operation, each of the other. One biocomputer interlocks with one or more other biocomputers above and below the level of awareness any time the communicational distance is sufficiently small to

bring the interlock function above threshold levels.

In the complete physical absence of other external biocomputers within the critical interlock distance, the self-directed and other-directed programs can be clearly detected, analyzed, recomputed, reprogrammed, and new metaprograms initiated by the solitudinous biocomputer itself. In the as-completely-as-possible-attenuated-physical-reality environment in the solitude of the void space, a maximum intensity, a maximum complexity and a maximum speed of reprogramming is achievable by the self.

In the field of scientific research such a biocomputer can function in many different ways, from the pure austere thought processing of theory and mathematics, to the almost random data absorption of the naturalistic approach with newly found systems or to the coordinated interlocks with other human biocomputers of an engineering effort.

At least two extreme major kinds of methods of data collection and analysis exist for individual scientists exploring interspecies interlock. They can use the artificially created, controlled-element, invented-devised-system methods or they can employ the participant-observer interacting intimately experientially methods with naturally given elements with nonhuman or human biocomputers as interacting parts of the system. The first kind of method is the current basis of individual physical-chemical research, the latter kind is one basis for individual explorative discovery-research with large-brained organisms like humans, dolphin and whales.

I sought sets of human motivational and procedural postulates for the interlock of research with and on beings with biocomputers as large and larger than the human biocomputers. Some of the methods I sought were those of establishing long periods—such as months and years—of human-to-other organisms biocomputer interlock of a quality and value sufficiently high to merit interspecies communication efforts on both sides at an intense and dedicated, highly-structured level.

Retreats From Interlock

SOME HUMAN SCIENTISTS FACED WITH NONHUMAN SPECIES who have brain-computers equal to or larger than their own retreat from responsibilities of interlock research into a set of beliefs peculiar to manual, manipulating, bipedal, featherless, recording, dry, air-vocalizing, cooperating-intraspecies, lethal-predatory dangerous, virtuous-self-image, powerful-immature, own-species worshipping primates, with 1400 gram brains.

Specifically, human scientists faced with dolphins—with 1800 gram brains—retreat into several safe cognitive areas, out of contact with the dolphins themselves. The commonest evasion of contact is the assumption of a human a priori knowledge of what constitutes scientific research on dolphins, which is a limited philosophical, species-specific, closed-concept system.

Common causes of retreat are fear of the dolphin's large size, of the sea, of going into water, of the Tropics, of cold water, and so on. The experimental mucking around of "let's see what happens if we do this" is another safe retreat. Years can be spent on this area with no interlock achieved so that successful evasion is thus continued endlessly.

> Human scientists faced with large-brain dolphins retreat to safe cognitive areas, out of contact with dolphins themselves.

Increasingly scientists endorsed an ethnological approach of "let's pretend we are nonexistent to the dolphins observers and do a Peeping-Tom-through-underwater-windows on them." This activity also evades interlock research quite successfully.

Other cognitive traffic control devices to evade the responsibilities of close contact with another species appear about as rapidly as each additional kind of scientist enters the arena with the dolphins. Ichthyologists, zoologists, comparative psychologists, anthropologists, ethnologists, and astronomers each have had at least one representative of their field approach dolphins. Each thinks up good and sufficient reasons for not continuing interlock research and not devoting resources to such far-out, non-applied, long-term, basic research. Non-scientist-type persons also approach and most leave with similar sophistries. A few stay. Some who stay have an exploitative gleam in their eye—dollar-gleam, military-application-gleam, self-aggrandizement-gleam. Some persons stay because of a sense of wonder, awe, reverence, curiosity, and an intuitive feel of dolphins themselves.

Dedication to dolphin-human interlock without evasions is a difficult new field of exploration. The dolphin respecting—not dolphin-loving—scientists are the potential interlock group sought. The persons I knew in this class were few. The few need help—facilities, assistance of the right sorts, privacy, few demands, money, cognitive and intellectual backup, encouragement, enlightened discussions—and dolphins, of course. It is necessarily a lonely pursuit.

Metaprograms for Interspecies Interlock

SEVERAL AUTHORS HAVE PROPOSED MODELS of human and nonhuman communication based on purely logical, linguistic, and technological grounds. Such models suffer from one major defect—they lack the necessary experience with interlock research with a nonhuman species in the proposer of the model. The model is defective because the storage banks of the theorizer are filled only with human-type interlock data. Of course this does not mean that these models are totally inapplicable. It merely assures a subtle pervasive anthropocentricity that may be inappropriate.

Among many possible theoretical approaches is one which I call a *participant theorist* approach. In this approach theorists establish interlock with a nonhuman biocomputer by whatever modes are possible. They then programs themselves with open-ended hypotheses of a type thought to encourage themselves as well as the other-species biocomputer to communicate with one another. The resulting interactions between the two biocomputers set up new programs, driven by metaprograms that may establish communication with the other-species biocomputer. The new theory develops with the new data as each evolves in feedback with the other. Corrections are introduced in context almost automatically by reward-punishment interactions in response to errors on each side of the interspecies dyad.

Evidence of Interlock

TURSIOPS TRUNCATES, BOTH BOTTLE-NOSED DOLPHIN AS THEY ARE POPULARLY KNOWN, HAVE A BRAIN known to be sufficiently large to motivate the human end adequately. It has been found with Tursiops truncates that a large daily commitment of hours, on the order of 16 to 20 hours of the 24, to interlock is necessary for the human end. The days per week must be at least five, and preferably six or seven. After 11 weeks of these hours, an approximate total of 1000 hours of interlock, the communication achieved via nonvocal and vocal channels is quite complex. At the human end, the theories are quite new and operationally successful, from an order take-orders level to several higher levels.

With dedicated interlock the conscious-unconscious reciprocal models of each species' biocomputer in the other-species become workable within the limits inherent in each participant. The limits set are also conscious-unconscious—at the human end at least.

Such interlock participation and realistic model building and rebuilding avoid the sterile purity of the armchair approach. It assures interlock in most areas, including some interlock even in those areas forbidden to western so-called "civilized man". The total necessities in each mode of expression are presented irrespective of taboos, inhibitions, bad theories, and blocks in either species. Areas to be loosened up are indicated unequivocally by each member of the dyad to the other by powerful methods. If communication attempts by one side are blocked in one area by the other, search tactics are employed in many cases until an open channel is found or until a channel is developed suitable to each end.

Establishing Rules

MUTUAL RULES ARE ESTABLISHED EARLY in the interlock to regulate the muscle power and force to be used, and areas considered dangerous, the "absolutely" forbidden areas, the first channels to be considered, the limitations on the use of each channel, who is to have the initiative under what conditions, the contingencies surrounding feeding and eating, around sexual activities, arriving and leaving, sleeping, urination and defecation, the introduc-tion of additional members of either species, and the use of props and evasions. The initial phase of sorting out the dyad's rules consumes most of the initial 1000 hours of interlock.

Consciousness-Unconsciousness

THE CONSCIOUSNESS-UNCONSCIOUSNESS ASPECT of the initial period of interlock is an important consideration. If too much hostility-fear is present unconsciously, the interlock becomes ritualistic and evasive. If the human end has too much unconscious energy involved in unconscious circuits of dependence on humans of the mother-child-father variety, fear-hostility may rupture the interlock. When powerful means of clearing out the unconscious excess-baggage circuits are used, I have seen an access to inter-lock of a depth and energy previously lacking in that human. A willingness to participate at all levels effectively is generated and used as the biocomputer is cleared of unreasonable circular feedback programs operating below the level of awareness. This is at the human end of the system.

At the other-species end of the system, the selection of individuals for interlock is more hit or miss. We caught dolphins in the wild. We don't know how they selected—or if they did select—the group for us to catch. There seemed to be some selection going on. Rarely did we catch very old dolphins. Most of the individuals we worked with had none of our unconscious-hostility, unconscious-fear programs in their dolphin biocomputers—at least not in the hands of our people in the Institute.

It may be that dolphins cannot afford waste of the unconscious circuitry for such useless programs as hostility-fear to intelligent other individuals. The conditions for their survival in the wild require the utmost in fast and unequivocal cooperation and interlock with one another. The exigencies of air-breathing, of sharks, of storms, of bacterial diseases, of viral illnesses, of man's depredations, and of other risk factors require exuberance and whole-hearted participation from each and every individual. Failure to interlock because of fear, hostility or other inner preoccupations leads to quick death and nonpropagation of that type of biocomputer.

Dolphins, correctly approached, seek interlock with those humans who are secure enough to openly seek them in the sea water. There are possible and probable interlock channels for humans with dolphins. Anatomical differences limit the channels, as do human social taboos. There are many channels, given a human with minimal inhibitions, the necessary sensitivity, skills in the water, courage, dedication, correct pro-gramming, and the necessary surrounds and support,

including sound production-hearing; muscular-action-tactile-
pressure-reception; presence-action-seeing; sexual-affection;
feeding-eating; and such meta-channel problems as initiative in use, cross-channel relations simultaneously with
intra-channel control of signals, and kinds of signals
which can and cannot be decoded into information at
each end.

Mimicry

WE DISCIPLINED OURSELVES AND THE DOLPHINS to pursue the
airborne vocal and hearing channel. In this channel we
found a clue to progress in the other channels. To be
convincing in regard to showing that a program and
metaprogram wish to communicate, we mimicked the
dolphins' signals even though at first the signals made no
sense. Similarly, we insisted on having our own signals
mimicked on the same basis. This lead to the dolphin
mimicking our swimming patterns, for example, after we
had mimicked theirs.

Mimicry seems to be one program for demonstrations
of the present state of the model of the dolphin in us
and of us in the dolphin. The adequacy of the functioning of the human in the man-dolphin interlock is measured by the feedback represented by mimicry. The mechanism is similar if not identical to that of a human child
mimicking adult use of words—silently or vocally—not yet
in the child's "storage" and "use" programs.

Plea for Further Research

A PLEA IS MADE for the development of a theory of the
human-type communicator faced with a nonhuman communicator with a brain and presumed mind of a high
quality. The theory should include open-ended, non-
species-specific, general purpose, self-programming, mutual
respect, voluntary dedication, participant theorist kinds of
basic assumptions. Beyond these assumptions are those of
the proper selection of participants, support, interest in
the scientific community, and cooperation on an operating
contributing level by open-minded professionals.

19
Metaprogramming Body Image

 OME OF THE MOST DEEPLY ENTRENCHED and earliest acquired metaprograms are those of the personal body image of the human biocomputer. Among the programs of importance here are those of posture, walking stance, sitting patterns, lying down patterns and body posture during sleep. This metaprogramming interdigitates with acquired muscular skills of every sort, including writing, running, skiing, sports such as tennis, swimming, and so forth. These metaprograms also interdigitate with programs for the use of the body during highly emotional states such as angry outbursts, sexual activities alone and with a partner, fright and flight patterns, and so forth. The self-metaprogram feeds back on itself through the external body image seen in a mirror and through proprioceptive and postural feedbacks.

To investigate the proprioceptive and muscle tension aspects the body image requires deep probing of programs combined with attempts to push every joint of the body beyond the limitations set by the current self-metaprogram. During such maneuvers to increase the range of motion at specific joints, you quickly discover the joint capsules and muscles themselves have assumed anatomical limits that attenuate the range of possible motion at these joints. This is particularly true of the spinal joints and the pelvic joints with the spine and with the femur. Similar considerations

> Body image metaprograms are deeply entrenched.

apply to the rib cage and the thoracic spine, the cervical spine, as well as, the limb joints. By daily repeated regimes of reprogramming of the muscles and the joints, it is possible to begin to modify these entrenched programs.

In the entheogenic state it is possible to program in positive system activity. Under these conditions the net effect of stretchings and muscle exercises can be a positive system excitation and reinforcement of the new patterns. During the entheogenic state it has been noticed that the activities of the negative systems are attenuated and thus allow a greater range of muscle and joint stretching than without the entheogen. It has also been noticed that it is possible to contract the desired muscles more fully in this state than during the usual state. Caution must be observed, however, because it is now possible to contract muscles to the point where muscles, joint capsules, ligaments, and tendons can be strained leaving residual, unpleasant local pains after the primary entheogenic state is ended.

By looking at the body image in a mirror while exercising in the entheogenic state it is possible to detect the supra-self-metaprograms for the body image—both the positive and the negative ones. You can see the negative metaprogram, for example, as the projection of an aged and crippled body assumed to be too old to be capable of changing the body image. A positive projected metaprogram might be that of an athletic young figure, for example.

Certain kinds of negative attenuation and zeroing-out metaprograms are connected with pelvic movements. If there is a supra-self-metaprogram directed against the movements of sexual intercourse, these are reflected in body posture and in the range of use of the pelvis in other activities. Such metaprograms can be detected in the projected images, placed upon the mirror image of the body itself, by watching the posture of the projected image and the range of programmable functional movements of the pelvis.

> You must hold and dissipate anxiety to metaprogram programs maintained by fear.

The imagined dangers of sexual mating can be seen by the failure of this set of images to go through the full ranges of such motions. Reprogramming such anti-metaprograms requires the real body to go through the "forbidden" movements in order to investigate the anti-metaprograms. Generally, this requires extreme exaggeration of the real body movements in order to break through the inhibitory aspects of the undesired metaprogram. Individuals vary from one another in the essential details, even as their metaprograms vary.

Face the Fear

A CERTAIN WILLINGNESS TO EXPERIENCE that which is feared most is absolutely essential as a basic metaprogram in order to achieve the new body image programming.

Cautions are in order here to avoid the narcissistic-self-worshipping-evasion of reprogramming in this area. The new areas of experience opened up can be rather seductive of themselves, because of the enhanced positive system activity during the entheogenic state. The necessity for regression and regrowth from times at which the natural developments were stopped can lead to further sticking of the metaprogramming at an earlier age on hedonistic grounds. Additional supra-self-metaprograms insisting on a natural evolution of the self-metaprogram towards a desired set of ideal metaprograms is necessary here to assure progress.

In older persons with well-developed characters these dangers are not as pressing as they are in younger subjects. However, the self-metaprograms involving the body image are also more entrenched in older persons. More energy and dedication to the task at hand are needed in older persons.

In those in whom obesity has become a problem, it is necessary to reduce the body weight to a more ideal level while carrying out these exercises in remetaprogramming of the body image. In other words, it is necessary to carry out those real dietary and exercise instructions which lead to a real externally better body in the sense of physical health. Such a regime can reduce the probability of the onset of the typical diseases of old age, with increasing health and activity.

More Rewarding.

ONE METAPROGRAM WHICH HAS BEEN WORKED OUT in great detail which may be of help to some persons is the set of exercises and dietary rules commonly called Yoga. These exercises assure new areas of stretching and new areas of breathing exercises which can enhance the physiologic functions of lungs as well as somatic musculature, joints, bones, and posture. In many ways these exercises assure adequate massage of the heart and blood vessels in such a way as to increase their activity along healthy lines. It may be that the probability of a coronary attack, angina pectoris, and similar problems of the aged can be reduced with yoga. Obviously other organs are also participating, including liver, kidneys, spleen, and so forth.

In obesity the panniculus adiposes—the large fat store in the omentum and in the mesentery—severely limit function of all the viscera and limit the amount of stimulation that can be given these organs through exercise. Such large fat reservoirs also require very large amounts of circulation of their own and hence require an increase in blood pressure to force that circulation. Thus the external changes in the body image are reflected in internal changes throughout the body, in a self-reinforcing manner.

20

Perception and Belief Interactions

NDER CERTAIN SPECIAL CIRCUMSTANCES it has been found possible to program certain trends in perception and project them into the visual space for study. Among such processes are the apparent presence of other beings. Belief in the reality of these presences is not at stake here. We can detect that they are not existing in the external reality, unless we purposely intensify the belief in the reality of these presences. The sensible metaprogram is that they exist only in the mind even though they appear to exist outside the body.

We may ask if these programs exist continuously below the threshold of consciousness in the usual mental state, or are they created de novo in or by the entheogenic state? In the psychoanalytic and psychiatric view they exist in the "unconscious" below the levels of awareness and are evoked from that region of the computer by the entheogenic state. All we can say here is that this looks like the more likely of the alternatives. However, other alternatives should be kept in mind.

Some of these below-threshold-programs once detected within the entheogenic state can be detected near threshold in a highly motivated state in solitude without use of an entheogen. Without entheogens we can achieve the necessary excitation of these programs to force them above threshold.

Experiment with a Migraine

IN ONE SUBJECT migraine was used as an advantageous tracer and a spur to the self-analysis. In this case there were asymmetries of the spatial perception fields. The right side of the visual field was very different from the left side so that what was seen with the right eye was different from that seen with the left eye. These differences were evident in color, in the persistence of after images, in the occurrences of scotoma during a migraine attack and so forth. The clinical literature indicates that such conditions can exist easily forty years or more. Among these asymmetries there are spatial distortions of the visual system. In this case the right eye was more sensitive, had a lower threshold for photophobia and for pain in general. The sensations and skin perceptions on the right side of the head were less pleasant and stronger than those on the left side. The migraine attacks were confined to the right side of the head.

At times correct programming can be achieved in the entheogenic state so that these cephalic differences can be enhanced, studied, and projected. Recall and living out of past experiences from childhood show a traumatic use of the right side of the head. The patient experienced abrupt physical blows to the right side of the head with violent shrinking away from the source, with right eye closure falling away to the left, and brief apparent "loss of consciousness." This is an example of a long-term apparently built-in unconscious program. The experience was elicited with the help of the LSD-25 state and the help of abreactions in classical psychoanalysis. All that was seen of this program during the usual daily external reality state was the asymmetry of perception.

"As If" Presences

IN THE LSD-25 STATE the migraine patient's autonomous program generated some presences not real but perceived as if real. When this effect was raised above threshold with proper metaprogramming, the presences were felt and seen as shadowy creatures or persons coming in from the right side of the visual field out of darkness. The impression was that the spatial field of perception became distorted in such a way that the presences could penetrate the distorted field.

When discussing this effect, the patient generated a theory of the projections as if it were no projection. The patient stated that they were beings from another dimension penetrating through a hole between their and our universes. This attribution of causes makes no sense unless it is believed implicitly, of course. When the intensity of belief in this system was lowered, the critical thresh-old for the distortion of the perceptual field became obvious and the unconsciously programmed projection process became detectable. The artificial beings were no longer that, they were merely distortions of the visual field because of some peculiar development of the nervous system. The dramatic bringing in of external beings was shown to have a need of its own, a relief from the solitude and isolation. Essential loneliness gave rise to the creation of the beings within this particular person. The necessity of projecting his anger and fears through the creation of these beings was found in the subsequent analysis.

Contemplation in the Void

STUDY OF THESE PHENOMENA after these experiences in the solitude and isolation of the void space without using an entheogen showed that the distorted field can be detected by relaxation of vigilance and by free association into the edges of the perceptual spaces using any random sequence of stimuli for the projection energy. The beings or presences did not appear without the entheogen, however. Peculiar distortions of the perceptual space did appear. These distortions gave the excuse for the projection of the beings. The patient created alien presences out of perceptually distorted noises by means of a belief program. The complex patterns of the noise coming through the spatially distorted and modified fields of the perceptual apparatus allowed creative construction of figures which satisfied current needs.

These distortions of the field were not static. The effects, which were maximal to the right, were seen as time-varying functions. Not only was there an apparent geometrical factor fixed to the body coordinates but there was a varying set of factors. It was the latter set that were locked in by an unconscious program for perception and for feelings. Beliefs for the metaprogram determined the outcome of the evocation of these programs in the entheogenic state. The patient said to himself, "The presences seen come from outside me and my program storage." These metaprogrammatic orders were used in his computer to construct and modify whatever apparently came in to create presences and at the same time to place the presences outside the computer.

Thus, we see that metaprogramming orders were used twice—for constructing a basic belief about the external reality of the presences and for a display which demonstrates the results of computations using that belief. The belief was used on incoming signals with uncertain or distorted origins. The patient found it practically impossible to program such projections without the entheogen. He could not use this basic belief to counter the powerful external reality program. It might have been possible for him to use this belief in other extreme conditions, such as in the presence of white noise of large magnitude, in the hypnogogic state, in the dreaming state in sleep, or during hypnotic trance.

The patient said, "With the usual high levels of daylight in the summers or artificial light in the house, with the stimulation of me by other persons, with the usual high sound levels of external reality, all organized in demanding ways to call upon purposes integral to me, I cannot—or will not—program alien presences in the external reality. Nor will I any longer so program 'presences' into other persons, as a consequence of my detection of the fact that I unconsciously programmed presences of my own creation to other persons."

Belief Projection

IN MOST CASES the unconscious programming is used to project our own beliefs and "presences" into and onto other persons in the external reality. This is the easiest route to use and the hardest to detect. The detection is difficult because of (1) the resemblance of one human to another, (2) the apparently meaningless "noisy" signals other persons emit in every mode, and (3) the interlocking feedback relations between the self and the important persons in the external reality or the apparent but effective external reality created by telephone, radio, television, motion pictures, books, and other idea transmitters.

Patients can thus have evocable proof (false) of the reality (false) of their beliefs about another person. It is almost as if we can extend our own brain-computer into that of another person by feedback and thus use the other as an actor, acting "out there" the part assigned by our

> Unconscious programming is used to project our own beliefs other persons in the external reality.

own beliefs. Naturally, the performance is not perfect.

It is difficult to see these processes when the roles are accepted by the other and unconsciously acted upon as new programming. On the other hand, if the other person opposes the assigned roles, we have an opportunity to examine these processes in our self.

Self-Assumptions

WE CAN MAKE THE FOLLOWING SELF-ASSUMPTIONS about the above sources of information gathered in solitude in the void space, and/or in the entheogenic state. They originate (1) inside our own head; (2) from other beings, nonhuman; (3) from outer space intelligences; (4) from ESP with humans.

Transcendence program

MODERN SCIENTISTS ASSUME that information comes only from self, such as from storage wholly within the human biocomputer. But there are, in fact, other potential assumptions. Programming can be assumed to have come from self, or from other humans, and/or from other beings. Each of the assumptions needs to be empirically explored—which is a challenge to science.

21
Positive-
System State

ROM THE IDIOT: "For a few moments before the fit", Dostoyevsky wrote to the critic Nikolai Strakhov, "I experience a feeling of happiness such as it is quite impossible to imagine in a normal state and which other people have no idea of. I feel entirely in harmony with myself and the whole world, and this feeling is so strong and so delightful that for a few seconds of such bliss one would gladly give up ten years of one's life, if not one's whole life.

Prince Leo Nikolayevich Myshkin: "He was thinking, incidentally, that there was a moment or two in his epileptic condition almost before the fit itself (if it occurred during his waking hours) when suddenly amid the sadness, spiritual darkness and depression, his brain seemed to catch fire at brief moments, and with an extraordinary momentum his vital forces were strained to the utmost all at once. His sensation of being alive and his awareness increased tenfold at those moments which flashed by like lightning. His mind and heart were flooded by a dazzling light. All his agitation, all his doubts and worries, seemed composed in a twinkling, culminating in a great calm, full of serene and harmoni-

*ous joy and hope, full of understanding and the knowl-
edge of the final cause. But those moments, those flashes
of intuition, were merely the presentiment of the last
second (never more than a second) which preceded the
actual fit. This second was, of course, unendurable.
Reflecting about that moment afterwards, when he was
well again, he often said to himself that all those gleams
and flashes of the highest awareness and, hence, also of
'the highest mode of existence', were nothing but a
disease, a departure from the normal condition, and, if
so, it was not at all the highest mode of existence, but,
on the contrary, must be considered to be the lowest.*

*And yet he arrived at last at the paradoxical conclusion:
'What does it matter that it is an abnormal tension, if
the result, if the moment of sensation, remembered and
analyzed in a state of health, turns out to be harmony
and beauty brought to their highest point of perfection,
and gives a feeling, undivined and undreamt of till then,
of completeness, proportion, reconciliation, and an
ecstatic and prayerful fusion in the highest synthesis of
life?' These vague expressions seemed to him very
comprehensible, though rather weak. But that it really
was 'beauty and prayer', that it really was 'the highest
synthesis of life', he could not doubt, nor even admit the
possibility of doubt. For it was not abnormal and
fantastic visions he saw at that moment, as under the
influence of hashish, opium, or spirits, which debased
the reason and distorted the mind.*

*He could reason sanely about it when the attack was
over and he was well again. Those moments were merely
an intense heightening of awareness—if this condition
had to be expressed in one word—of awareness and at the
same time of the most direct sensation of one's own
existence to the most intense degree. If in that second—*

that is to say, at the last conscious moment before the fit–he had time to say to himself, consciously and clearly, 'Yes, I could give my whole life for this moment,' then this moment by itself was, of course, worth the whole of life. However, he did not insist on the dialectical part of his argument: stupor, spiritual darkness, idiocy stood before him as the plain consequence of those 'highest moments'. Seriously, of course, he would not have argued the point.

There was, no doubt, some flaw in his argument–that is, in his appraisal of that minute–but the reality of the sensation somewhat troubled him all the same. What indeed was he to make of this reality? For the very thing had happened. He had had time to say to himself at the particular second that, for the infinite happiness he had felt in it, it might well be worth the whole of his life.

'At that moment,' he once told Rogozhin in Moscow during their meetings there, 'at that moment the extraordinary saying that there shall be time no longer *becomes, somehow, comprehensible to me. I suppose,' he added, smiling, 'this is the very second in which there was not time enough for the water from the pitcher of the epileptic Mahomet to spill, while he had plenty of time in that very second to behold all the dwellings of Allah.'*

Convulsions of Orgasm-Like Type

If convulsion (behaviorally seen) includes prolonged hyperactivity of (+) systems, convulsions act as positive reinforcement with increased seeking and repetitions of ways of repeating the experience–as concluded from observations and research of Dostoyevsky, Bickford, Sem-Jacobsen, Lilly.

22
Major
Metaprograms

External Reality Metaprogram

THIS METAPROGRAM OPERATES PROGRAMS with inter-lock with the outside-body-systems. These systems include all of external reality. Human beings are a defined part of the external reality.

The external reality metaprogram seems to be always present, except when in special states and, even then possibly is only relatively attenuated but not completely absent. The states in which the external reality metaprogram is attenuated include sleep, coma, trance, anaesthesia, and so forth. Such states cause centrally conditioned reductions of the stimulation arriving from the external reality. It is also possible to attenuate the external reality stimuli themselves.

In the profound physical isolation of the void state, external reality excitation of the CNS is attenuated to minimum possible levels in all modes. If in profound physical isolation, one adds a metaprogrammatically active substance to the brain such as a powerful entheogen, further attenuation of the external reality stimuli can be achieved and the ego—self-metaprogrammer—is more fully activated. If in profound physical isolation of the void state you add sleep, trance, or light levels of anesthesia, these give external reality cutoff and cessation of external reality excitation of the central nervous system—and of the "mind."

The external reality metaprogram is increased in its intensity in high excitation states. Interlock with the external reality can be increased by creating a high excitation state—chemically with an entheogen or electrically through a seizure.

2. Self-Metaprograms

SELF-METAPROGRAMS INCLUDE ALL OF THOSE ENTITIES which are usually defined as ego, consciousness, self, and so forth. The interlock of the self-metaprograms with the external reality metaprograms can be attenuated by special techniques including sleep, use of powerful entheogens plus isolation, anaesthesia, and so forth. The apparent strength of self-metaprograms can be enhanced in certain cases by a powerful entheogen plus dextroamphetamine, and other psychic energizers.

3. Storage Metaprograms

STORAGE METAPROGRAMS HAVE TWO ASPECTS. In the active storage process inputs from external reality and from self are connected to storage. Secondly, in the active output process the self is connected directly to storage. Search programs achieve these connections. The nature of storage programs vary depending upon special conditions. They vary in free association states, hypnogogic states, dreaming states, and other altered states of consciousness. Entheogenic agents allow a special state in which the self-metaprograms can consciously explore the storage itself. In this state of expanded consciousness the self-metaprograms and the search-metaprograms operate coextensively in such a way as to reveal the innermost files of the storage directly to self.

4. Autonomic Programs

THE AUTONOMIC NERVOUS SYSTEM has built-in properties that are programmatic rather than metaprogrammatic. These autonomic programs do not exist directly in self-metaprograms. The relationships between these and the self-metaprogram are second order. Autonomic programs include the programs for the gastrointestinal tract, for sex, for anger, for fright, and so forth. These programs can be modified by the self-metaprogrammer. Biofeedback is a good tool for accessing autonomic programs. Once started their detailed carrying-out is automatic.

5. Body Maintenance Programs

BODY MAINTENANCE PROGRAMS CUT ACROSS the lines of the autonomic programs and include such conscious- unconscious programs as the needs and the carrying out of sleep, exercise, correct food, environmental temperature regulations, clothing, and so forth. The realities of the body maintenance in the external reality are included in these programs.

6. Family-Love-Reproduction-Children Program

THESE PRIMARY RELATIONSHIP PROGRAMS are an aspect of the external reality metaprogram.   They are one of the basic external reality program.   There can be many more programs depending upon the individual computer. Some may be devised as above, others cut across the above boundaries. Such divisions are artificial and reflect the tendency of a human to think and act disintegrated into categories rather than as an integrated smoothly operating holistic computer.

7. Survival Metaprograms

SURVIVAL PRIORITIES ARE USED IN CASE OF THREAT to the structural or functional integrity of the entities named. The order is that of relative importance in the sense that the one below in the list will be sacrificed, abandoned, penalized, or changed in order to save, maintain, integrate, or educate the one above in the series.

A "threat" is defined as internal or mental information, which when above threshold anticipates and predicts immediate or delayed destruction, mutilation, confinement, abandonment, damnation, ostracism, solution (lysis) of continuity, compromised integrity, moral encroachment, severe ethical insult, voluntary seduction, unconscious entrancement, slavery, and so forth.

In nonthreatening educative processes the listing is more flexible. Any entity may, for a time, be placed at the head of the new list. This survival priorities list may remain intact in this order in the depths below awareness. It is evoked in states of fatigue that begin to generate information above the threat threshold.

0. The Soul-Spirit Programs

THE SOUL-SPIRIT CONCEPT includes life after mortal death, reincarnation, the immortal entity, that which is God-given, none of which is recognized in current Science. Some persons consider soul-spirit as the most valuable of all the available entities. Depending on the needs of the definer, this entity may be educable, may have higher ethical strivings than current ones, may store information of certain kinds, may develop skills in certain areas, may carry these capabilities within it to the next state after the current mortal physical reality is left, and so forth.

1. Ego-Mind Entity Programs

ONE'S MIND AND MENTAL SELF are valued above the body and in those with the above religious belief, below the soul.

2. Body Programs

IT IS OBVIOUS THAT WE VALUE OUR BODIES less than our mental self. However, at times we can be forced to act as if the list did not have this order but the opposite. Sometimes the mind shuts down, leaving the body to its survival battle alone.

3. Lover Programs

STARTING WITH THE PROTOTYPIC FATHER and mother models and moving to wife or husband models.

4. Child Programs—One's own child.

5. Sibling Programs

6. Parent Programs

7. Valued friends Programs

8. Humans in General. Programs

Glossary

Communication

THE PROCESS OF THE EXCHANGE OF INFORMATION between two or more minds. Communications also refers to the process of exchange of information between metaprogramming entities within two or more computers.

Information

THE CALCULATED MENTAL RESULTS of the reception of signals from another mind and the computed composed context of the next reply to be formed into transmissible signals. Information also refers to the data received, computed, and stored resulting from the reception of signals by a metaprogramming entity from another computer and the computed data in the ready state in the same entity for transmission to another computer through a similar set of signals.

Mind

THE ENTITY COMPRISING ALL—at least potentially—of the self-detectable processes in a brain which are at such a level of program complexity as to be detected and at least potentially describable in programming language. The mind is the sum of the self-metaprograms within the brain. It is a form of metaprogram in the software set of a very large biocomputer which organizes metaprograms for the purposes of self-programming and of communication. The mind also refers to the computer-brain-detectable portion of a supra-physical entity tied to the physical-biological apparatus. The mind is the remainder of this entity is in the soul-spirit-God region and is detectable only under special conditions.

Program

A SET OF INTERNALLY CONSISTENT INSTRUCTIONS for the computation of signals, the formation of information, the storage of both, the preparation of messages, the logical processes to be used, the selection processes, and the storage addresses all occurring within a biocomputer, a brain.

Metaprogram

A SET OF INSTRUCTIONS, descriptions, and means of control of sets of programs.

Self-Metaprogram

A SPECIAL METAPROGRAM involving the self-programming aspects of the computer to create new programs, revise old programs, and reorganize programs and metaprograms. This entity works only directly on the metaprograms themselves, not the programs. Metaprograms work on each program and the detailed instructions therein. Alternative names include set of self-metaprograms, self-metaprogramming entity, and the self-metaprogrammer.

John
Cunningham
Lilly, MD

OHN LILLY WAS BORN THE SECOND OF THREE surviving sons to prosperous Catholic parents from St.Paul, Minnesota. Early in childhood he encountered intelligent "Beings" during a life-threatening illness and on other occasions. Such experiences give evidence of a precocious self-awareness already wrestling with the contradictory tensions between a fully realized internal world and the social constraints of the external consensus reality.

As a sixteen-year old student Lilly wrote a sophisticated essay posing the question "How can the mind render itself sufficiently objective to study itself?" This question continued to intrigue Lilly throughout his long career, as first, a brilliant research scientist using a neurophysiological approach and, latterly, as a pioneer explorer of the frontiers of human consciousness using whatever tools he could find or otherwise invent.

Following initial studies in neurophysiology at the prestigious California Institute of Technology, Lilly graduated as a medical doctor from the University of Pennsylvania in 1942. Invited to join the faculty, he spent the war years applying his inventive technical skills to

> At 16, John Lilly wondered how the mind could be sufficient objective to study itself.

high-priority Air Force research. Following his "My body is my laboratory" principle of never subjecting another to any experiment he wouldn't first perform on himself, Lilly acted as the guinea-pig in a dangerous experiment studying the effects of explosive decompression on pilots at high altitude.

Established at the cutting-edge of neurophysiological research, Lilly was invited to Washington to work at the National Institutes of Health. This strategic move gave him status in two opposing camps, the National Institute of Neurological Diseases, staffed by specialists in the physical brain, and the National Institute of Mental Health, staffed by those interested in the *mind*. Lilly experimented on living brains using novel techniques he developed, which allowed him to stimulate monkey brains without major trauma and without damaging the brain tissue. With this methodological breakthrough Lilly became the first scientist to locate the brain's pain and pleasure centres. Military interest in his pioneering work for less benign purposes, however, caused Lilly to change tack.

Consciousness Research

IN THE 1950s, neuroscience was unable to determine if brain activity was an intrinsic organ function, independent of stimuli from the outside world. Lilly set out to test if the brain would shut down when no stimuli were received required isolating the brain from all sources of sensory input. Employing the novel technique of floating the body in a supersaturated saltwater medium maintained at body temperature, Lilly demonstrated that the brain remains active, even when deprived of external stimuli. In fact, long hours spent floating in "the tank" gave Lilly access to profound states of physical relaxation in which the mind became active in unanticipated ways and presented the observer with colorful images, memories, waking dreams and unusual

Lilly demonstrated that the brain remains active, even when deprived of external stimuli.

levels of consciousness—including a sense of contact with other intelligent "Beings." Lilly's scientific peers were less than enthusiastic, partly because the results were necessarily subjective–whatever *that* meant, and largely because Lilly had broken through the boundaries of the prevailing scientific paradigm.

These amazing experiences made Lilly wonder if other consciousnesses existed that might be utilizing these physiological benefits of floatation. Such questions led him to consider marine mammals–dolphins, porpoises and whales–the majority of which have brains that are larger than humans but are morphologically similar size and of an equivalent level of neuronal complexity. Lilly wondered if the cetacean *brain* might not also contain a *mind*. Study of dolphins' vast range of elaborate signals supported the growing evidence that dolphins were endowed with language and logic capacities. If so, then why not thought? Why not a sense of self?

Research into the possibilities of communicating with the cetacean mind was to occupy Lilly for the rest of his working life. After leaving the NIMH he set up a series of pioneering laboratories that analyzed human-dolphin communication over the next 20 years. This ground breaking research promoted worldwide interest in dolphins and whales as intelligent life-forms and was fundamental to establishment of the Marine Mammal Protection Act of 1972.

Entheogens as a Portal

FOLLOWING HIS FIRST EXPERIENCE WITH LSD-25 in 1963, Lilly became a tireless researcher into psychotropic substances as a portal into the mind—and beyond. The results were revolutionary. From then on Lilly advanced brain/mind research, which combined the tank and government-approved LSD experimentation to provide provocative data on the self-observing mind, while continuing his work on communication with dolphins. The results of his LSD-based research for the NIMH were published in a 1972

> John Lilly was one of the 20th Century's great scientists.

monograph, *Programming and Metaprogramming in the Human Biocomputer*, a significant work that has been called the *Principia Psychologica* of the Cybernetic Age and from which this book evolved. After LSD became illegal in the late 1960s, Lilly experimented with Ketamine, which he substituted for LSD and is chronicled in his "metaphysical autobiography"—*The Scientist*.

John Lilly's wonderings about the intelligent "Beings" who appearing to an enraptured child set him on course to becoming one of the 20th Century's great scientists.

—Gerard A. Houghton

Afterword

ROGRAMMING THE HUMAN BIOCOMPUTER IS A BOOK to live with, to read and reread slowly over months, lingering days on some pages, pondering and imagining, interspersing reading with meditative and psychedelic explorations in whatever form of isolation you can create, ideally including flotation tanks. That's how I read the original edition during my freshman year at New College, in communion with peers going through their own personal psychedelic quests. Combined with Stan Grof's *Realms of the Human Unconscious*, a therapeutically-oriented book about the structure of Mind based on evidence from LSD research, John Lilly's research fundamentally changed my life and provided the inspiration to devote myself to founding Multidisciplinary Association for Psychedelic Studies (MAPS) and conducting psychedelic research.

In the midst of the maelstroms of those times, the integrity of John Lilly's ruthless intellectual inquiry provided a compelling hint of hope for the eventual triumph of science over superstition, for the promise of the power of courageous psychedelic introspection to penetrate through screens of projection into the depths of consciousness, mental function, and mystical/religious experience. Without having encountered John Lilly's work at that formative stage of my life, at a time when psychedelic research was being suppressed, ridiculed and belittled all over the world, I doubt I would have been able to see the central importance to science, politics and ethics of participating in the pitched battle over the use of psychedelics as research tools to explore the human Mind.

Programming the Human Biocomputer shines as a guidebook of great value permitting voyagers to engage in a structured and profound self-examination. If pursued to logical conclusions in a dispassionate manner, readers/voyagers can emerge with a grounded set of ever-evolving personal and political hypotheses, beliefs, identifications, and values.

Lilly largely adopted and worked within a classical psychoanalytical framework which is more intellectualized and less cathartic than the transpersonal psychotherapeutic approach developed by Stan Grof. To readers seriously engaging the ideas in this book, I wish to emphasize the importance of combining the intense elucidation of cognitive programs with an equally intense focus on working to understand, experience, clarify, appreciate, and purify one's own inner emotional life within a supportive context that values the depth and richness of emotions as much as cognitions.

> Shines as a guidebook of great value.

The essential importance of each of us doing our own inner work, and of John Lilly's masterful guidebook to that work, are stated starkly and clearly by John Lilly himself. "One only has to look at the present state of Man's world, at the inadequacies of Man's treatment of Man, and see how far we must go if we are to survive as a progressing species with better control of our battling animalistic superstitious levels." In our personal and collective struggles to survive and thrive, John Lilly deserves enormous gratitude for the courageous, pioneering work.

–Rick Doblin, Ph.D.

Multidisciplinary Association
for Psychedelic Studies

maps.org

Cultural, Cetacean, Scientific, and Academic Alliances

The John C. Lilly Archive resides at Stanford University at Stanford, California.

For further research:

www.johnclilly.com

www.soundphotosynthesis.com

www.samadhitank.com

www.ace.to

www.floatation.com

www.pcrf.org

www.biospherefoundation.org

www.theoctobergallery.com

Printed in the USA
CPSIA information can be obtained
at www.ICGtesting.com
JSHW022341140824
68134JS00019B/1613